DISCOVER YOUR SUPERPOWERS:

The Key to Unlocking Your True Potential

For permissions requests, write to the publisher, addressed "Attention: Permissions Manager," at the address below.

Ordering Information: Quantity sales—Special discounts are available on quantity purchases by corporations, associations, and others. For details, contact the Special Sales Department at the address below.

Publisher: Your True Potential
Address: 3982 Powell Rd Suite 148 Powell, OH 43065
Web Address: www.yourtruepotentialcoach.com
Telephone: 614-987-8320

Library of Congress Control Number: 2018914216

Discover Your Superpowers/Tamara Paul
1. Non-fiction—General
2. Non-Fiction-Self-help
3. Non-Fiction-Inspirational
4. Non-Fiction-Motivational

ISBN: 978-1-7326838-0-8

Printed in the United States of America

10 9 8 7 6 5 4 3 2 1

Discover Your Superpowers:

The Key to Unlocking Your True Potential

Tamara Paul

DEDICATION

This book is dedicated to my children, Tito Paul II and Trey Paul. My precious time with you gave me the inspiration to write this book. My husband Tito Paul Sr., for encouraging me to grow and live my best life, and to my mother, Charlmel Simmons, for using her superpowers and leading by example.

ACKNOWLEDGEMENTS

I'd like to acknowledge my business partners, Manika Glass and Dr. Keisha "Kee" Fletcher-Bates, for sharing the vision and journey with me.

My literary consultant, Joylynn M. Ross for her guidance.

Assistants, Rose Black and Misti Mazurik, for their support.

Kathleen Ventura for assisting in the superhero research.

Manju, Adam, and Brian, for holding down Rep Network while I concentrated on the book.

Nicole McNair, Joshua Ross, Veronica Wilson, and Tiffany Vinson for mentally digging deep with me.

Michele Washington, for allowing me to share her heroic story.

Donna James, for bringing out some dormant superpowers in me.

Whitney Barkley for bringing the vision to life.

Nicole Marie Ricart for your amazing photography.

Steve Ruhs, Andrew Herman, Joel Londen, and JL Woodson for their inspirational creativity.

I'd like to acknowledge my family for your inspiration, guidance, and for allowing me to see your superpowers in action, because my story wouldn't be as powerful if I hadn't witnessed it for myself.

In loving memory of my sister-friend, Tamiko Brown
(January 14, 1976 – December 7, 2018) who powered
through a battle with cancer for five years. Tamiko's
superpowers of love and compassion, patience, giving,
genuine loyalty, strength, and gut intuition was shared with
and received by many. I love you, sis!

TABLE OF CONTENTS

INTRODUCTION

*I*n your lifetime I'm sure you've heard someone say, "I'm not a superhero, I'm only human." Perhaps you've said it yourself a few times. But what if, in fact, you are a superhero? You've simply yet to unlock your superpowers? You've simply yet to reach your true potential in every area and on certain levels of your life?

I've known I had a powerful message to share since I was a teenager. The vision was loosely in the back of my head. I'd see myself presenting, conducting seminars, and mentoring young adults. More times than once I've said to myself, "The messages that come to me—the messages inside of me—can't just be for me." The experiences I've had in my life were so obviously planted that they had to be shared.

Throughout the years, I've unknowingly or subconsciously been mentoring friends, family, and occasionally a stranger or two. The problem with my vision was I couldn't see the entire picture. I couldn't visualize the concept and had no idea what I was supposed to say, or even do, in order for the vision to manifest fully. It was tough knowing I had a message, but not knowing exactly what to do with it in order for it to reach the masses.

A couple years ago, the urge got stronger for me to do something with the message, so I started soul searching and asking myself lots of questions. I needed to put the pieces of the puzzle together. I discuss in this book the final piece to that puzzle. The final piece I've been waiting for. It's the piece I waited 20 years for!

Yes, I finally figured it out, and now it's time for me to share it. This tool—this resource—that you are holding in your hand, is the blueprint! It's the blueprint to help you set new intentions for your life. Within these pages is the key to ignite the power within you, a power that will allow you to soar to your true potential in life. A power that will help you decode those messages (thoughts, ideas, concepts) that are either lying dormant within your very being, or stirring in your soul like a ladle; your visions, talents, gifts, skills, dreams, and goals . . .

the gumbo . . . the soup . . . the dish that's been brewing inside that it's time to serve to the world on higher and the highest of levels.

I initially got my coaching license because I thought my purpose was to help people one-on-one, but shortly after receiving my certificate, the messages started flowing with an intensity that wouldn't let up—that wouldn't calm or rest in my spirit. It was evident to me that these messages were not just for the handful of people I could reach with one-on-one techniques. These messages were supposed to be shared with many people.

Discover Your Superpowers: The Key to Unlocking Your True Potential will allow you to dream with intent, work harder, believe more in yourself, realize it's not too late to change directions, make better decisions, and capitalize on your surroundings. I will discuss briefly the backstory of various superheroes, and then discuss how it applies to our human powers, and how you can use these powers to reach your true potential.

So, wrap yourself tightly in your proverbial cape, and let's soar!

Introduction

Discover Your Superpowers

CHAPTER 1
MANIFESTATION AND TRUSTING THE PROCESS

Wonder Woman, AKA Diana Prince, is a superhero. She's a god. No, seriously, she's a god. That's part of her origin. I imagine being considered a god could go to some people's head, but not Wonder Woman; it goes to her heart, unlike Iron Man, whom we'll discuss later.

Wonder Woman is compassionate, vulnerable, and a divine feminine believer. She has the power of belief like no other superhero. The same way one's spiritual God may be referenced to as love, the same goes for Wonder Woman in her role as a god to her cosmos.

Each and every last one of us, like a superhero, has a backstory, one that shapes who we are, how we love, and that which develops our capacity for giving and sharing. Our backstory dictates decisions we make for ourselves, whether good or bad. Taking a look into your backstory and truly understanding your past can shape your future. It is my hope that as you read each chapter of this book and are either introduced to or learn more about the immortals referred to as superheroes, that you will have a desire to uncover your own 'why' and dig deeper into your backstory. But for now, let's discuss Diana's.

Diana was raised on Themyscira, a fictional, lush city-state and island nation, by the queen of the Amazons, Hippolyta. Diana's identity as a goddess and daughter of Zeus is kept from her so that Ares, the god of war, might not find her and destroy her. Does anything about Diana's backstory thus far relate to yours? Has your identity been kept from you in some way? Was your father's or mother's identity not known to you, or was it in question? And were "justifiable" reasons the cause of your identity being withheld from you? Were you made to feel the truth would have destroyed you, when in fact, it was not knowing the truth that may have caused the most harm?

It can be quite difficult to know who you are and where you are headed if you have no idea where you came from. Iyanla Vanzant once said that in order to know who we are fully, we need to know who our parents are, as we are an extension of them. Knowing them or even knowing a little bit about them plays a part in our backstory.

Knowing who she is and where she came from, Diana eventually leaves the Amazons and Themyscira to fight in World War I with Steve Trevor, who she ultimately falls in love with before his untimely death as a soldier. Before his demise, together they fight to end the war, and they succeed. Have you ever felt like you left a place of comfort and security (home), only to find yourself feeling like you were fighting a war in order to survive outside of your comfort zone? A war with others? A war in which perhaps you were your own enemy? If so, what was the outcome? Did you stand strong in defeat, or did you return to your comfort zone feeling overcome? Being vulnerable is not always easy, and that's typically what being outside of our comfort zone leads to; vulnerability.

Although Wonder Woman is compassionate and vulnerable, she is strong and fierce, commanding respect as Wonder Woman *and* Diana Prince. It's amazing that whether in work mode or not, Wonder Woman didn't shrink inside herself. She didn't lose herself in either her role to her people (family), or the world (her job). She didn't see herself as less than in either aspect. How admirable!

Seems as if she's got it all together in the eyes of both worlds, right? After all, she's a god with powers to do what may be impossible for others to achieve. Does it sometimes seem as if, to the outside world, you've got it together, so you make every effort to uphold that appearance? Looks can be deceiving, especially if we can dress them up to the point where what's beneath is almost unrecognizable or simply concealed.

I think most would agree that Wonder Woman's exterior, her outfit, in the words of Beyoncé, slays. All superheroes have tools and weapons, but Wonder Woman's ensemble commands the room. Not only is it intriguing, but everything she dons has a purpose.

Her Lasso of Truth forces anyone it captures into honesty. The Bracelet of Submission is indestructible and represents loving submission and the emotional control associated with it in order to balance out the strength of the human ego. Her Projectile Tiara is a symbol of Wonder Woman's status, and can be used as a weapon, similar to a boomerang. Her sword is a god killer, which led Diana to the realization that she was a goddess (self-discovery). Her shield is used for protecting and deflecting (ummm . . . the irony).

Break down your exterior and discover how it might relate to your interior. What part of your exterior is a symbol of your status? It doesn't have to have a physical connection; for instance, it can be a car, house, fancy watch, or designer handbag. Do you use it as a weapon; throwing around your weight, so to speak?

How do you use your power suit/exterior? For good or bad?

Although Wonder Woman has her areas of strengths in which make her seem invincible, she does have weaknesses. It's not as if she hides them. They are just as evident as her superpowers, only our eyes tend to focus on the exterior. Without all the bells and whistles (tiara, bracelets, etc. or jewelry, shoes, etc.), Wonder Woman can be rendered powerless to a degree.

What happens when you take off your power suit? Are you still powerful, commanding respect? Are you still honored and loved? More importantly, do *you* believe that you are still powerful, honored, and loved?

When it comes to what one believes in—the act of believing—some may not see this as a superpower, but to me, it's one of the greatest powers on Wonder Woman's repertoire. Her power to believe before she sees the actual manifestation is unparalleled. What's in your heart, and do you see it in your mind before it ever manifests? Do you believe in the manifestation before the actual manifestation?

Wonder Woman doesn't need to know the exact 'how' and the exact 'when' of what she believes in her heart; she simply believes. We all have the superpower of manifestation, and with a plan behind it, we are fierce!

I first saw the quote "If the mind can conceive it and the heart can believe it, then you can achieve it" when I was a teenager. Without even knowing exactly what it meant and how powerful the statement truly is when it comes to manifestation, I quickly adapted it into my life.

Have you heard of the law of attraction? I like to explain the law of attraction as the three "W's":

- Want
- Wait
- Work

The three W's equal manifestation.

Manifestation is a powerful tool we all have. It's one of our superpowers. Some know how to activate it better than others, but we all have the capability. We often manifest things in our life without even knowing it.

To break it down so you can understand exactly what manifestation is, I'll sum it up like this: Manifestation is the power of <u>wanting</u> or believing something so much, and knowing in your heart and soul that it will happen, so much so that you're <u>waiting</u> for it to happen. You're not hoping it happens. You're not wishing it happens. You know it's going to happen . . . so you wait for it to happen—you wait for it to manifest, all the while putting in the necessary <u>work</u> needed to complement the manifestation, and for you to be prepared for it as well. It's not simply saying to yourself, "I'm not sick," believing it, and waking up the next day feeling great. This may require turning up the heat, taking your vitamins, etc., AKA work.

My youngest son manifests things all the time. He talked about a keychain he wanted for his backpack for two weeks straight. I worked hard looking for the keychain, because I knew he wasn't going to forget about it, and that he wasn't going to rest until he had it in his hands. He literally spoke about it every day.

I happened to take him and my oldest son to the store with me one evening, which I rarely do because they are five and eight years old, and getting them out the store without additional unnecessary items is next impossible. This just happened to be a day I was feeling brave. Lo and behold, guess what my youngest son saw in the check-out line? Yep, the keychain! Not just any keychain, but the exact keychain he'd been talking about for weeks. He'd been wanting it. He waited for it, never doubting he'd get it. I even worked hard looking for it; just as hard as he'd been searching himself. Then he got it.

To be honest with you, I wasn't even surprised. He gets fixated on things he wants, and it's like they magically appear.

The example I just gave above is a simple example, I know, but the point I want to make is that we do this manifestation thing naturally. You manifest all day long. Imagine what you can do if you actually put practice behind it—if you do it with intention—and do the work to back it up.

I definitely have manifested my thoughts and beliefs into existence, and would love to share multiple experiences with you, but to avoid boring you, I'll share one special moment that changed my life forever.

I went into labor at 17 weeks with my first child, which required me to stay in the hospital four months. I was a pharmaceutical sales representative at the time, but still had dreams of becoming an entrepreneur. I knew the exact type of business I wanted to own and operate. Two of my friends came to visit me in the hospital and we were having a discussion around business ideas. It was sort of like a think tank session where we discussed business ideas and opportunities. We all had big dreams and loved sharing them with each other. During that session, I kept saying to them over and over that we needed to find a medical supply company that had a product but didn't have a salesforce to push the product. We could start a company that would bring them the salesforce they'd need to promote their products to various physicians.

That idea stuck in my head, and during my hospital stay, I did a great deal of research on manufacturing sales reps and manufacturing companies. I was searching for products and networking with people who were in this business already. I knew there had to be a company with a product out there in the marketplace that needed a salesforce. Over the next year, I continued my networking and my search for products without any doubt that I'd eventually find them. The second year, I prepared myself for when the opportunity would present itself. I created a business plan around recruiting sales representatives, the onboarding process to get them hired, and training to ensure all sales representative delivered the same message.

During the waiting process, I was continuing my education, training, and networking, but about three years later, I did receive a call about a company that had a product but no salesforce. I was then able and in position to provide them with one.

Some would call it a coincidence, but it wasn't. My vision and belief manifested itself. I took the thought that surfaced in my head as well as the hardcore belief, and then mixed it with hard work, research, and preparation . . . and it happened! You can't tell me we don't have superpowers!

Let's talk more about manifestation and the power of positive thinking. Do I wholeheartedly believe we all have this gift? Absolutely! I recently heard Oprah's speech about her obsession with the movie *The Color Purple*. She purchased the book for her entire staff, then the next thing she knows, she's getting a call to audition for the movie. It wasn't a coincidence or because of her name; she manifested that audition. What a powerful example!

Let's specifically talk about the third 'W' in manifesting desired outcomes; Work. Are you prepared to put the work into getting your desired outcomes in life? Not only does it take work to manifest, you also need to be prepared for when the opportunity presents itself. What do I mean when I say it takes work to manifest? Well, our minds can play tricks on us, so staying one step ahead and in control of our inner thoughts alone is work. It doesn't stop there, as there is additional mental work involved.

If you have an idea or thought of something you truly want in your life, you have to want it with every muscle, tendon, vein, organ, and blood vessel in your body. More importantly, your mind needs to want it.

You have to feel like it's already done. You need to be thankful it's coming, which is the waiting part, but you also need to know it's going to happen and PREPARE for when it does. Being prepared takes work. This is the hard part, because, again, the mind plays tricks. It takes confidence, guts, ambition, and the ability to fight the conscious mind; the mind that's telling you not to be a dreamer; the mind that's telling you you're not good enough; the mind that's programmed to believe in limitations; the mind that's programmed to come up with excuses; and the mind that's feeding off of your backstory. You're on the right path if you can get the negative thoughts out of your path. Don't forget to get the negative people out of your way while you're at it!

For me, vision boards have been a huge part in my manifestation process. My children, who are in grade school, have vision boards. Their vision boards are full of toys, but they do have blankets for the homeless on there as well.

What is a vision board?

A vision board is a tool used to help clarify, concentrate, and maintain focus on a specific life goal. The vision board is the "if the mind can conceive it" part of my favorite quote. Being able to visualize what you want is just as important as putting the plan together to get it. Note: my vision boards are not just for show. I put action behind them.

You must be able to see yourself riding around in the new car in order to manifest a new car. You need to be able to visualize yourself sitting and drinking coffee in your new home in order to manifest the home. Call me a daydreamer if you want, but those daydreams allow me to check off items on my vision board. Don't judge until you've tried it, my friend.

I create six-month vision board goals. This allows me to check off what I've completed and attach a new goal. There are multiple vision board apps for computers and cell phones. Google "vision board app" and take your pick! My vision board is my screen saver, so I have a constant reminder of my goals.

Once you've accomplished your goal or dream, you can officially say you manifested it. My vision board shows me the path to completing the goal. For example, if I want to purchase a new car, it will take for me to save additional money. So, on top of the picture of the car, I will put a picture of a piggy bank with the amount I need in the bank to purchase the car. Once I've collected the money, I can take off the photo of the piggy bank, and my new goal of the car is underneath. This allows me to focus on the money and not the car. If you want a new car, you must add the action steps to ensure you get the new car. The universe will help you get the money by giving you an increase at work or freeing up time for a part-time job, but it's your job to save for the car.

The vision board is a great tool for visualizing, but you have to believe in the manifestation of it. I've written ad nauseam about believing in your thoughts, but believing means you have to be enthusiastic about your role in acquiring the vision and be intentional about what you're asking for.

A friend of mine attended a conference, stood

up, and introduced himself as a millionaire. Now he wasn't a millionaire at the time . . . but he is now. If you combine the three W's—want, wait, and work—then there is nothing holding you back from accomplishing your largest and greatest goals. There is nothing holding you back from being who you desire to be.

Someone asked Wonder Woman who she is. Her response, "A believer."

Are you a believer? I'm not merely referencing being a believer on a spiritual level. But are you a believer in your dreams, your goals, your visions and desires? Are you a believer in yourself? You don't get what you hope or wish for, but you can get what you believe or want.

Everything that you can conceive, you can be. Use your imagination. Be intentional with your thoughts. If you have the capacity to dream it, then you have the power to make it come true. You have great power that was given to you as your birthright. You cannot have what you're not willing to become.

It wouldn't be right if I only spoke about the positive side of manifestation. Your thoughts don't only have power when they are positive. Negative thoughts (villains) have power as well. If you are a negative thinker, it's vital you practice to change your mindset.

Do you know that person who says, "If anything bad is going to happen, it will happen to me, because I have horrible luck?" I can think of a few, and bad luck happens to them all the time. Why? Partly because they manifested it.

You are so powerful that the universe hears all your directives. And unfortunately, it picks up on the negative ones as well. It's life, so negative things will happen, of course, but it's your responsibility to get over it quickly and accept that nightmares don't last long. You eventually wake up from them.

If I have a bad morning, I will shift the energy by saying, "Wow! This morning was pretty bad, which means this afternoon will be terrific." I recall on one occasion telling my mother how the start of my year had been so horrible for me, that the second part was going to be so phenomenal that one day I'd laugh about the details of the first part. And you know what? I did!

Look back at those bad moments and find something great about them. If you're stuck in traffic due to an accident, which makes you late for work, instead of being horrified that you're in traffic and will have to hear your boss's mouth, switch the energy and say, "Thank you for making me late today, because it could have been me in that accident if I had left a few minutes earlier."

If you have a glass of water and the water level is in the middle, do you say your glass is half empty or almost empty? Have you ever thought about looking at that glass as if it's half full or almost full? If your glass is half empty, then your mindset is going to need to change, and you can change it.

The power of the mind is so strong that if you constantly are telling someone they are a pain in your neck, then when the pain hits, don't wonder where it came from. You might think, "Tam, that was a stretch." But is it?

Pay attention to what you say and how you say it. Look for the positive in all situations. Ask for good change to happen. Feel that, that change is coming. Believe that positive things are coming your way.

If you're thinking right now to yourself, *Does manifestation really work?* If you are doubting yourself and your power to manifest already, then we have some work to do. But all good things come to those who put in the work. Knowing that you already manifest every day of your life, what is wrong with doing the work to learn how to do it in a positive way to get what you want?

Throughout the remainder of this book, we are going to discuss multiple superheroes and their superpowers, which in turn, will make you more aware of and get in touch with the superhero in you, and to unearth your superpowers within as well. The one thing you're going to need to do is trust the process. There's no magic, hocus pocus, twitching of the nose and bouncing of the head like *I Dream of Jeannie* and then, BAM . . . all your wishes come true.

There are no tricks, and I've not concocted any "too-good-to-be-true" techniques and strategies. Just as with manifestation, the process has always existed around you, but more importantly, inside of you. I'm simply going to show you how to navigate the process, and in doing so, I'm not going to instruct you to do anything I haven't done myself to hit benchmarks in my life. I've used the process I'm sharing with you and have seen many others use it as well to get what they want out of life by reaching their true potential.

This book is the vehicle, and the process is the chauffeur that is going to get you on the path toward your true potential. It's your responsibility to trust your designated driver; the process.

While we are speaking about trusting the process, in doing so, you must have patience that not everything will happen when you expect or when you feel it should happen. As a matter of fact, ask yourself this question: "Am I ready for it when it happens?" And for starters, you don't always have to know exactly what it is. Just know that it is (if that made sense). Like Wonder Woman, simply believe.

I constantly announce to myself, "I'm so excited about what's about to come my way, and I am thankful, ready, and willing!" I don't necessarily know of the it that's coming my way, but I'm grateful for it, nonetheless.

I do hope this is all making sense to you. But in short, trust the process of what it may take to reach your destiny, and exercise enthusiasm about the process.

While I take pride in my power to manifest, I have also mastered the art of trusting the process and being enthusiastic about it. That means when things don't go my way, I accept and believe that it didn't go my way for a reason. If I have my heart set on something and it doesn't happen, I am comfortably okay with the outcome.

One of the most powerful moments in my life of trusting the process was when I was interviewing to be the breast implant rep for one of the largest device companies in the world. I had dreamed of being a device rep from the time I got into pharmaceutical sales. It was the next step for

Discover Your Superpowers

me in taking my career to new levels, and I knew I would achieve it one day. So, when I found out the position was open in my city, I immediately tracked down a former coworker who I knew worked for the company that was offering the position. I contacted her because I figured she would know the hiring manager and be able to give me some pointers, which she did.

I drove an entire hour to the interview, and during the interview, I knew I was doing an amazing job. I was so confident. I was fricken unstoppable! I had the interviewers' undivided attention. These men were hanging onto every word I was saying.

After nailing that interview, I got in the car and called my husband as I drove back into town. I remember telling him how well the interview had gone. I also told him that if I didn't get the job, then it wasn't meant for me to get it; that it was meant for one of the other interviewees. But deep inside, I knew there was no way anyone could've done a better job interviewing for that position than I had. And I trusted that if I did not get the job, then something even greater awaited me.

I found out the next day that I was right; I did interview better than everyone else, per the manager, but he still gave someone else the job, because that person had management experience and I didn't. My confidence didn't change one bit. I knew that I hadn't gotten that job for a reason. But I also knew something greater awaited me.

The same former coworker I'd contacted to give me some pointers for the breast implant interview contacted me five months later and presented me with an opportunity I'd been wanting, waiting, and working for. I'd come to realize that connecting with her had nothing to do with the job I didn't get. I was supposed to connect with her because she was the "in" to my next big opportunity . . . that something greater that awaited me. I trusted the process and was patient.

Do you see how this worked out for me? I wanted the job so bad that I manifested the opportunity to get it. I trusted the process and had faith that if I didn't get the job, then it wasn't meant to be. If I would have gotten the breast implant job, I would have declined the opportunity presented to me five months later. The opportunity changed my life and catapulted me to higher-level benchmarks than I had set for myself, and all because I put my manifesting powers to work and trusted the process.

You must be enthusiastic. Enthusiasm is faith in action. Be enthusiastic about the decisions you make, whether it's buying a new car, entering or leaving a relationship, or deciding what to prepare for dinner. Be enthusiastic about what will happen as a result of that decision. And if the result isn't exactly what you envisioned, then be enthusiastic about the something greater that's in store for you.

Speaking of higher-level benchmarks. If you are dreaming the dream, don't be surprised if your dreams go beyond your expectations. Just because your mindset is on level five doesn't mean your dream can't hit level ten.

My husband and I would drive around for hours in a particular neighborhood, dreaming of upgrading our home to that area. We knew one day we would move to that neighborhood, and we did. A nearby community took our thoughts to a level we couldn't comprehend. We didn't have the capacity to dream that big. We admired it from afar and stayed in our mental lane. But guess what? We now live in that neighborhood.

We made the mistake of not dreaming big enough. We couldn't stretch our minds to believe or dream that big. We couldn't see past the first house, but a bigger dream awaited my family. And my goal is to help you reach higher levels by dreaming big and using all your resources, tools, and superpowers to make it happen. Believe in big things. The dream is meant for you. Bow down to it and let it become you!

As easy as it is for Wonder Woman to want and believe, it is equally as easy for you. Release the death grip on your hows and whys, when, whats and wheres, and take hold of the possibility and reality that it just is . . . that it can, and will be done.

CHAPTER 2
SLOWING DOWN AND FINDING BALANCE

To describe the superpowers of the superhero, The Flash, quickly (pun intended), he's the fastest man alive. He also has advanced healing powers. Geesh; some people don't feel as if they were blessed with one ability, let alone two. How does one become so fortunate? Perhaps learning a little bit more about The Flash will provide some answers.

Although there were several individuals who played the role of The Flash, let's focus on one. Barry Allen, known as The Flash, received his powers when a lightning bolt struck a case of chemicals in his lab where he was working. As a result, the chemicals rained down and reacted with Barry's body. When he came to, he'd suddenly been equipped with the ability to move at the speed of lightning.

Have you ever felt not only as if lightning had struck your life once, but twice? How did you react to it? Did it make you better, stronger and wiser, or did it make you bitter, angry, and hindering? I'm certain Barry wouldn't have thought being struck by lightning and then doused with chemicals that could have killed him would have an upside. Oh, but it did! Can you find the upside to the disaster that may have happened in your life—perhaps even on your job, just like with Barry?

Barry always wanted to be the hero; not necessarily a superhero, but a hero nevertheless. Most people do strive to be the good guy; the person who saves the day; always helping and never setting out to harm anyone. But often we find ourselves in situations where we are challenged to do the right thing . . . to say the right thing. We're often challenged to not fight fire with fire, or, as some say, give the ol' eye for an eye and tooth for a tooth, but to, instead, take the high road. A lot of times, the way we react to things has to do with how much weight we are carrying around, and how much more we can take before the straw breaks the camel's back (or our spirit).

Barry grew up living with a neighbor after

his mother was murdered and his father went to prison. What a heavy burden for someone so young to carry! What's unfortunate is that many people carry their childhood burdens into their adult lives, such is the case with Barry. He carried the weight of his mother's death with him. Can you identify weight from your childhood that you may have carried into your adulthood? If so, why are you holding onto it? If not, how did you manage to let it go?

Out of all the various Flash characters, Barry wasn't the fastest, but he was the strongest. So even though there were others with the same skills, gifts, and talents as Barry, there was still something unique about him that stood out. In our careers, especially with entrepreneurs, there are often thousands of other people doing the same thing we do. Our audience or customer is their audience and customer, and it often feels as if we are in constant competition. But just like The Flash, there is a trait, characteristic, or skill that sets us apart from others. On the flip side of the coin, just as it is with The Flash, we may have our disadvantages as well.

With The Flash, if he runs too fast, he can run into the past and change history, or he can end up trapped in the speed force. Superpowers must be exercised properly—no showboating!

Overexerting or overextending can cause more harm than good. For example, writers are told they should write every day, and it's been proven to be very beneficial advice. But as one of my fellow literary colleagues stated, "I write every day, not all day. This author has a life!" Dedicating our every waking moment to our job (even our goals) could result in missing out on other pertinent things in life, like spending time with our spouse, children, family, and friends.

The Flash couldn't get out of the past because he kept going in a circle, or "looping." Looping in the coaching world is going from the present, to the past, then to the future. It's not staying in the present. Fixating on the past can be detrimental, such as using the past as an excuse, then making bad decisions based on the past.

Slowing down and finding balance or ways to manage the various components, aspects, and details in our lives can be the difference between living in the past, which can ultimately blur the future. My future looks something like this: retirement years where I can get out of the rat race, working when and only if I want; visiting family and friends; traveling the world; playing tennis; working on hobby projects; getting spiritually grounded; recycling, retirement checks, and feeling the effects of financial freedom.

Why can't we have part of the same experience prior to retirement age? We can, actually. I'm not saying it's easy by any means, or that it can be done in a flash, but it can be done.

I'm not exactly sure if I am what would be considered a type A personality or Type B, because I resonate with both. Type A and Type B personality theory describes two contrasting personality types. In this theory, personalities that are more competitive, highly organized, ambitious, impatient, highly aware of time management and/or aggressive are labeled Type A, while more relaxed personalities are labeled Type B.

If I had to lean toward one or the other, I'd say I'm pretty heavy on the Type A because of the daily juggling act I perform. I'm married with two boys, CEO of one company and COO of another. I run a real estate company, I'm a life coach, treasurer of multiple associations, and I'm writing a book (published author by the time you read this); yet, I manage to find time for family, friends, meditation, exercise, and church. I might get behind in some areas, but I still squeeze in the *Young and the Restless*. Again, the balance I have didn't come easy. Balance is a choice and takes practice.

Here are a few things I do daily to help with

balance that may help you as well:

1. Look at your calendar and compare it to your vision board. Are you working on items that will help you achieve your immediate goals? Be protective of your time. If I'm not doing something that will help me check off a goal, then I'm not spending my time wisely. If you have to ignore calls, then so be it. You have work to do.

2. Set your intention for the day and keep a gratitude journal (we discuss gratitude journals later in the book).

3. Eat foods that give energy (leafy greens, whole grains, bananas, nuts, leans meats, fatty fish, beans and fruit).

4. Work out the same time and day(s) each week.

5. Schedule time for friends and family.

6. Schedule time to relax, meditate, or sit and just breathe deeply at least 10 minutes a day. It's just 10 minutes . . .

7. Drink lots of water (pay attention to your body when you drink water, and be aware of the changes).

If we constantly focus on going as fast as we can, growing, progressing, climbing the corporate ladder, and always "onto the next," we may find ourselves somewhere we don't want to be and unsure of how we got there, i.e., with a successful career but no loved ones around us, or our health is in the gutter. Like my same author friend who I quoted earlier stated, "What good is financial wealth if your relationships are broke(n)? If your health—body and mind—are broke(n)?"

The Flash always has to be the over-the-top good guy, and his uncompromising moral compass can often create problems. Remember, a compass signifies balance, and not having it can create problems in your everyday life. The Flash is constantly fighting himself and he doesn't even realize it until after the fact. Don't allow yourself to spin in circles. You have to be fast enough to get out of your own way.

Finding balance helps you enter into true peace and happiness and you have the power to find it. It's one of the things we are all striving for, right? If I had a dollar for every time someone said to me, "I just need some peace in my life" or "I just need to find balance," I'd have lots of dollars! We make it harder on ourselves than it is. Prioritize, map it out, and do it.

One thing that helps me is mapping out my day the evening before. I'm old school, so I write on a piece of paper everything I need to accomplish the next day. Beside the item, I write the amount of time it will take me to accomplish it. I total up the hours and then fit it into my schedule. Now what works for me might not work for you, but at least you are thinking about it. Try various methods, written, typed or spoken, and find what works best for you. You can start by Googling "time management methods."

Figuring out what gets you off-balance sooner rather than later can be of great value. An imbalance can lead to stress, anxiety, a feeling of being unfulfilled, as well as frustration. Trust me; I've been there multiple times. The beauty of writing this book is that I'm not telling you anything I haven't experienced, tried, and in some cases, mastered. Then there are those instances where I failed miserably, but I can rest assured knowing that every experience has allowed me to understand what's needed, how to access it, and how to implement it. These experiences keep regrets at a minimum.

Regrets are a direct reflection of not having balance in your life. At the end of the week, are you feeling like something or someone got neglected? It happens, but there's always next week . . . when you commit to doing better. Choose to accept the decisions you made and make a plan on how you can avoid that in the future.

Your plan can be dividing your balance into two categories; inside and outside. Taking care of both is essential. The inside balance includes mental clarity, health, heart, and soul. The outside balance is family, friends, work, passions, and playtime. Now map it out. You can't focus solely on the outside and ignore your mental clarity, health, heart, and soul. Use your calendar to map it out. What are you doing week one to focus on family, friends, passion, and playtime? Add it to your calendar. Now, add in your meditation activities to help with mental clarity, exercise for your health and heart, and whatever you need to tap into for your soul.

Remember the importance of sleep. In order to prevent stress, anxiety, and unhealthy habits, you must be well rested.

Consider the word "adaptability" when you're walking through this journey. How do you adapt to change in your life? Because to use your dormant superpowers you will need to ignite change. Slow down and remember what it means to be human. Being too busy will make you compromise the basics of life. Balance in your life will help you remember to play.

Discover Your Superpowers

*C*HAPTER 3
*I*NTUITION AND *G*UT *I*NSTINCT

*T*he Daredevil is a superhero who happens to be blind. Let's be honest; there are some people who wouldn't consider a blind man as a candidate for a superhero. The thing about Daredevil is that his other four senses have such superhuman accuracy and sensitivity, most people don't even know he's blind. Those senses coupled with radar vision is what allows Daredevil to don the title of a superhero.

Isn't it great how even though we may lack in a certain area, the areas in which we excel in make up for it? Daredevil's abilities give him the confidence to fearlessly take on crime. Do you possess qualities that when you put them in action, you operate and move fearlessly in them? In the moment, they enable you to forget all about the qualities you may lack or fail to perform. When you are in a groove or zone implementing and executing your stand-out skills and techniques, you are simply unstoppable!

Even though Daredevil's inability to see may be considered a lack, it creates an overflow in his ability to listen. I tell people all the time, "Shut up and listen." We spend way too much time talking, telling, or asking for what we want, instead of listening to what we are supposed to be doing. It's important to be a leader, but in being a leader, you still have to discern when to lead a conversation, and when to simply be a part of it.

Pre-superhero, Daredevil was Matt Murdock, blinded as a result of a chemical spill that took place when he was a young boy. As we've discussed, Matt lost his sight, but he gained the following abilities, also known as superpowers:

Super-hearing: great listener

Super-touch: sense the body heat of others in close proximity, as well as their emotional state

Super-smell: recognize anyone by their scent, as well as tracking an individual smell

Super-taste: can tell what ingredients are put in his food

Are you a little disappointed? Were you

expecting me to share with you how Matt can fly through the sky, transport himself to other universes, or defend his galaxy with inhuman strength? For those who knew very little about Daredevil, you probably expected him to have superhuman physical abilities. Well, if it counts for anything, he did receive ninja training from a fellow blind man, but I'm sure most will agree there's nothing superhuman about that!

In spite of his lack of supernatural powers, he became a superhero nonetheless. One's physical attributes does not have to always play a role in their ability to achieve and excel. Do you or do you know anyone with a physical disability, yet their other abilities make you blind to their disabilities? Are you getting the connection here? I hope so, because despite not having one of the senses that his enemies have, Daredevil kicks major butt! Don't allow the one thing you may lack to hinder the areas in which you have overflow.

There is one other thing I'd like to mention about Daredevil, and that's the fact that if there is too much noise or extremely loud noise, it overwhelms his senses and renders him useless and vulnerable. Think about it; because of his heightened senses, Daredevil has superb balance. If there is too much going on, it can put him at risk of losing his sense of balance. Too much noise in your mind can do the same to you. It's important to protect your mind and avoid the noise of life as much as possible.

The greatest lesson to be learned from Daredevil is how much he trusts his body and his intuition. He is extremely in touch with his senses, and connected to the world around him. He can't rely on what he sees. He must rely only on the things he cannot see. He goes with what some refer to as gut instinct.

What's your stomach say?

Are you paying attention to the feeling your stomach is giving you? It's telling you something. Are you quiet and still enough to be able to do a gut check? Are you listening? These are your superpowers; don't ignore them!

Is your life balanced or managed to the point where you trust every move you make to be beneficial? Are you mindful of each and every move?

Unless you've been living in a bubble, I'm sure you've heard about meditation. Meditation is a practice where an individual uses a technique, such as focusing their mind on a particular object, thought, or activity, to achieve a mentally clear and emotionally calm state. Mindfulness is a form of

Discover Your Superpowers

meditation. For those of you who may be lost, let me go into a little bit more detail about mindfulness and meditation.

Mindfulness is bringing your attention fully to one thing. Mindfulness is cooking and only being focused on the recipe ingredients, the smell, and the colors of the food. Mindfulness is having a conversation with a friend or family member and being completely present. It's playing with your kids or grandkids and they know they have your undivided attention. It's painting or coloring and only being focused on that.

There are multiple forms of meditation, but the most common is bringing your attention to your breath. It closes down the thoughts and makes you focus on just your breath. Regardless of which style you prefer, I recommend choosing one. Mindfulness is my favorite.

I have a story I want to share with you, because without practicing mindfulness, I wouldn't have gotten the idea to write this book. A couple years prior to me deciding to pen this book, I met with a lady in my network for lunch. I spent the entire hour telling her that I had a message inside of me to share. From the time I was a young girl, I had a desire to teach and share my wisdom and knowledge as it grew and developed. But for some reason, I couldn't figure out what exactly I was supposed to be sharing. After being hit with a series of questions, she told me, "Your story is in your childhood and the lessons you've learned to date."

I left from our lunch that afternoon feeling super positive and inspired, now with some direction at least, but the pieces to the puzzle weren't complete just yet. Over the last two years, I've had a few great literary ideas and started loosely working on them, but it wasn't until I was sitting in my kids' playroom watching a superhero movie with them that it hit me. It hit me so hard I got goosebumps.

A voice penetrated my spirit; *They are watching and idolizing these superheroes, and they don't even realize that they, themselves, are the true superheroes.* The voice was so loud and so dominant to what was going on at the moment that I couldn't ignore it.

Over the next few days, I kept hearing the same voice repeating the same thing. Finally, I allowed my own voice to do the talking: "Tam, stop ignoring this." It took me a few days to follow my own command, but then, again, it hit me. It was the final piece to the puzzle.

Please allow me to continue to share. People have always asked me to what I attribute my success. My answer has not once changed: "It depends on how you measure success."

For me personally, I've hit some benchmarks, but I have yet to hit success. I challenge myself by determining the reasons I'd hit those benchmarks. For me, the answer was simple: Because I feel like I am a superhero too.

That was the message! I am a superhero, and one of my superpowers is that I have the gift to see the potential in others that they don't always see in themselves. That had been the message I'd been searching for; the calling I'd been trying to hear clearly . . . to pull out the superhero in you! To help you discover your superpowers so that you can reach your true potential.

I don't hit my benchmarks because I'm special. I hit my benchmarks because I use my superpowers. I'm compliant to my calling. I pay attention to all signs, and I use my powers to stay on the path to reach my calling.

In that moment, I'd finally gotten it! I'd finally figured out the message I had buried in my head for so long. I now had the blueprint, and I went on a mission to make sure I provided you the blueprint to not only abundance, but to discover your passion and your purpose.

How many times in your lifetime have you asked yourself, "What is my life purpose? What is emerging in my life? What is my gift to share? Why am I even here on this planet?" These are empowering questions to ask yourself, and just like I did, be aware; always look for clues, signs, and symbols . . . just like I did. Constantly be in tune with the messages within.

Once you know the message buried inside of you, don't hesitate to release it . . . that's exactly what I did. I put the things in place and motion to begin the writing and publishing of my message. Even in my dreams, I am my own superhero, and I've been identifying myself as such to friends and family since I was a teen. I fly in my dreams to get away from people trying to attack the city I'm in. I breathe underwater when my island is being bombed. It took time, patience, and mindfulness to get to this place, but I finally developed the message. It was all because I was actually paying attention to the movie my children were watching. I was aware of the looks of admiration on their faces as they watched the superheroes; not working or looking at my phone, and not ignoring the messages and signs from within.

I want and need you to truly understand this same ability you have within you, and how simply you can operate it. Your passion and purpose are already designed and waiting for you. It's within you and just needs to be ignited.

Chase your passion. Chase your dreams. Chase anything but the money. The money will follow as long as you follow the right things.

What do you think you're here for? Don't block or resist what's specifically for you by not figuring out your purpose and passion. Have you ever asked your higher power what's the intention for you? What's the dream for you? Ask and then listen and watch. It's up to you to pay attention to the signs you'll be fed. By finding out your passion and purpose, you'll be able to take ownership of what's already yours. It's your birthright, and it's yours for the taking!

Discover Your Superpowers

CHAPTER 4
YOUR SELF WORTH IS IN YOURSELF

Sometimes it's not who you are, what you are, or what you can do that makes you stand out. In spite of popular opinion, sometimes it's not even what you know or who you know that provides the opportunities for you to shine. In all actuality, it's your ability to simply utilize specific resources and share the information with others. Think about it; most gurus and experts are branded as such because of the resources they bring to the table or who they have built themselves to be. It's not as much their wisdom, knowledge, and expertise as it is the delivery of those resources and how others can benefit from them that elevates their platform.

Have you ever considered that perhaps it's your environment, your surroundings, or maybe even the resources made available to you that makes you stand out . . . that is, if you're actually utilizing them? Take for example Thor, another superhero who, in his universe, is a god. Some may also see Thor as a god physically. As a matter of fact, right here in the good ol' US of A, he could easily be a finalist in the Mr. Universe bodybuilding contest. But Thor's physical appearance plays second fiddle to what truly qualifies him as a superhero, which is a hammer. You read that right; a hammer. Well . . . I guess not just *any* hammer, but a super cool hammer from another dimension that gives Thor great power. A resource, so to speak.

It is Thor's physique that enables him to utilize the hammer to its fullest benefits. Are you conditioned to use the resources made available to you to their fullest benefit? The hammer is practically indestructible, but there's a catch. The wielder has to be worthy, or else the hammer will be useless. I'm not sure if Marvel has ever made this case, but what if the wielder also had to believe they were worthy? That would be quite a stipulation to adhere to, wouldn't you agree? And not meeting said stipulation could lead to the three D's: disaster, disappointment, and discouragement. Okay, there's a possible fourth D: Destruction!

Have you ever taken on a really large task, one

you felt you needed a cape and superpowers to see through? You knew every resource you needed to pull it off was available, but you still lacked confidence. Often, we only perform where our level of confidence will take us. We're all hyped and geeked, and then . . .

I've had moments in my life where I questioned myself and my self-worth; "I'm not worthy, smart enough, witty enough, knowledgeable enough, etc." I've been in rooms with CEO's, COO's and CFO's, AKA C-Suite Executives who have extraordinary talents, big titles, status, inspirational messages, and who I felt belonged in that room way more than I did. I've told myself that I needed to stay in my lane. But in my mind, the lane I was referring to was the slow lane. I held the title of both CFO and COO of the company I represented in the room, but I'd find myself downplaying my role or title before anyone could judge me. I was judging myself faster and harder than anyone else ever could have, all because of my insecurities and questioning my self-worth.

Imagine one minute you feel as if you can save the world, then the next minute you're rendered useless, all because you don't have either the resources, the confidence to utilize the resources, or self-worth. And maybe you aren't conditioned to utilize the resources. All those amazing things you've been able to do in the past have become disabled all of a sudden, and for one reason or another, you now feel worthless.

Thor uses his hammer to fly. He does so by throwing it to wherever he wants to go while holding the handle. Your resources, too, can take you wherever you envision them taking you. But how far can you get without your resources? You've put all your confidence into your resources, but none in yourself. None in the natural gifts and abilities you bring to the table.

Let's assume your resources are other individuals. How far can you get on your own without them? Sounds to me like Thor is working with a double-edged . . . hammer. What about you? Are you so dependent on outside resources that you can't get to the level you need to reach on your own? That you don't know your true value? So, you stay attached to things that you shouldn't, simply because you feel they can get you to where you need to go? Pay attention to every person you meet, because it's for a reason, and it may only be for a season. They may actually not at all be the person to get you where you need to go, but they could actually be the person keeping you from getting there. While you're holding onto them, they are holding you back, because where you are headed, they simply don't belong.

I learned over the years from being in rooms with ultra-confident people that these people were simply using their superpowers like they should have, but I found myself feeling like I needed my business partners to make me look good during big moments. I put major stock into their superpowers without realizing they weren't doing anything in the moment I couldn't.

I had to learn and build the confidence to believe that what I brought to the table may have been different than their contribution, but I was still contributing something they could not. I have a resource within me that is just as powerful as what they have. It took me to be in multiple rooms to finally realize this, but once the message hit me, it hit me hard, and I want to share that particular message with you: People need what you have because they can't do what you're capable of doing and providing.

In life, as with Thor, depending on what outcome we want, we, too, must be physically and/or mentally prepared and conditioned in order to reach certain destinations. And no matter how gifted, smart, and talented we are, sometimes we need resources in order to win. But on the same token, we can't be dependent on everything outside of ourselves.

When Thor doesn't have his hammer, he either loses all of his powers and becomes mortal, or he loses half of them. Thor has, on many occasions, had his hammer destroyed and found himself feeling powerless. In these times where he could not rely on his resource, he learned of his innate, true power within. He is god of thunder after all, a contender to Hulk, and is capable of so much even without his hammer. He is made to be powerful, just like you are.

Thor has always found a way to restore his hammer, but it was important that he learned how to use all his potential, even when he doesn't have it. We all have what we need inside of us. You are exactly where you are supposed to be right now. The people you're meeting, the lessons you're learning . . . all perfect! You have to see it, and more importantly, choose it. It's your decision as to when, where, and how to act on certain situations. What good is having the blueprint to build something if you're not going to build it? It's like going to school for almost a decade to become a surgeon, yet you spend your years being a hospital volunteer.

I earned a degree in interpersonal

communications with a minor in psychology. When I left school, I had no clue what I really wanted to do, and I didn't know what I was good at. My first job out of college was in the temporary service industry. I had a multifaceted role where I would recruit and train employees, and I would also go out into the field to encourage companies to use temp services. In other words, I was selling the services.

I left the first company and was recruited by a second to do recruiting only. I found great joy in the recruitment process, and I was actually pretty good at it. The third staffing company I was with, I was hired to do 100% outside sales, meaning I was the person going into the companies introducing the opportunity of hiring temporary employees versus hiring direct.

After the horrific events of 9/11 happened, the temporary industry suffered, and I lost my job. At that point, I became determined to get into the pharmaceutical industry. Plenty of resources and outside sales experience helped me land a job within two months. I spent 12 great years in the pharmaceutical industry, and I loved every minute of the experience. At the end of my pharmaceutical career, I was let go with a three-month severance package to show for my hard work and dedication.

But wait—before you start feeling sorry for me: Two weeks before I received notice of being let go, I received a call from a former coworker about a company who had a product but needed a sales team for a pharmacy (Yep, that call I discussed in chapter one). Do you see the connection?

It was a career marriage made in heaven; recruiting, which I loved and had a major passion for, and pharmaceutical, which I also had a love for and had major resources to help me excel at the job. Some of those resources were, in fact, individuals. I'm grateful for those individuals, but even without them, I was able to thrive. I was prepared for the challenge. I had been groomed for this. I recruited a sales team of over 700 reps across the country, and the rest was history.

Whatever you are doing right now in your profession, you are learning something you need to know, or you are meeting the people you need to know. Use the experience to be great at something. You could be learning the skill to start your own business or grow your business. Or you could be learning the skill to get your next big promotion and close your next big deal. You could be meeting your business partner or the person to introduce you to something life-changing.

Every lesson, experience, and connection are

coming to you for a reason. Take notes and gather and store your resources just like a squirrel does with nuts. It's all about being prepared to use your resources when the opportunity presents itself. Are you prepared?

Thor has a single resource, and without that resource, he's limited. But being without his resource teaches him how to utilize his true potential. His powers lose value because he loses his powers. Even though he feels less valuable without the power that his hammer gives him, he grows even stronger without it, and he does not let the setback of a loss of a resource stop him from getting it back. And if you happen to be in a season of learning self-reliance and self-worth, realize that the hammer you once used to fly, like Thor, isn't yours right now for a reason. Maybe it's time to slow your pace and walk for a while.

Don't be afraid to follow the same pursuit as the squirrel, who gathers its resources from many places. Note that the squirrel, prior to making it back to his nest, stores the resources within itself (its mouth). What's stored inside of you makes you your greatest resource!

Discover Your Superpowers

CHAPTER 5
WHAT IS HOLDING YOU BACK?

Named Clark Kent after he was sent to Earth for his protection by his parents from the planet Krypton, Superman may be the only superhero in which you can sum up his superpowers in one word; everything! Getting his powers from Earth's sun, Superman is probably the most famous superhero there is. Growing up, when it was time to play superheroes, he was the first chosen, just like the biggest and fastest kid on the playground when it was time to choose teams for sports.

On the flip side, it's Superman's weakness that is also referenced most when discussing one's drawbacks and vulnerabilities. As a matter fact, the fictional substance, Kryptonite, is the most well-known weakness of any of the superheroes. When referenced by man, its name is interchangeable with the ultimate impotence.

Kryptonite is from Superman's home, the planet of Krypton. Imagine that—something from your very own home being the thing that renders you weak and unable to function; the thing the vexes your spirit, paralyzing you to the point of stagnancy.

Kryptonite was discovered in many different forms, each having their own unique effect on Superman. Do you have kryptonite in your life that comes in many forms? What are they and what effect does each have on you?

We can say, "I don't sweat the small stuff" or, "I don't let life get to me" as many times as we want, but if everyone would be honest with themselves, each of us could admit that we have something in our life that makes us weak, interrupts our focus, or knocks us completely off course. It may be a painful divorce, handling money, past trauma, a mother-in-law, financial loss, loss of a loved one, not finishing school, the inability to have children, past regrets, overeating, fear of letting others down, loss of career opportunity, an abuser, or an ex-partner. Kryptonite can even come in the form of our children.

Sometimes compartmentalizing is the answer, but living by the mantra of not sweating the small stuff and not allowing life to get to you is easier said than done. There is a huge difference between the two; one is saying (just talk), while the other is action (actually doing something). When something gets out of control, we have to tame it, set it aside, or cage it. Another word for that is "compartmentalize." We don't close the issue up in the drawer and forget about it. We go back to revisit it with a clear head so that we are in control of the situation, and the situation is not controlling us. Often times, we can find a way to live with it through forgiveness and growth.

When was the last time you had to compartmentalize? Did you perhaps have a very important meeting to attend or lead, but you'd just had a disagreement with someone? How did it affect your performance in the meeting? If it didn't, what did you do to keep from taking the situation into your meeting? How did you compartmentalize, or table it?

Kryptonite didn't only handicap Superman physically, it affected him mentally as well. I'm going to be vulnerable in the next few paragraphs and share my Kryptonite.

Growing up, I always felt that there was

something that rendered me weak mentally more so than physically. It wasn't until I became an adult that I would learn what it was, ADD, which stands for Attention Deficit Disorder. It held me back from reaching my true potential in my adolescent years, and has challenged my adult years. I recall the teachers telling me I was going to be in a special reading class because I wasn't comprehending my reading assignments the way most of my peers were. At fourteen years old, though, that didn't actually mean anything to me.

I struggled in every subject that required reading. I was good at math and writing, so I counted on those grades to balance out my poor history and science grades.

My mom shared with me how one of my elementary teachers told her not to worry about me, and not to let my grades define me. I wish I could find that teacher to send her flowers. Those words of encouragement gave my mom just enough strength to keep encouraging me.

My GPA wasn't good; it was horrible, in fact. But I had two full-blown business plans written by the time I was 17. I wasn't what people considered book smart, but my cognizance and creativity were overcompensating for it, which gave me hope.

I knew my ideas, thoughts, and dreams were way

outside the box, but I still wholeheartedly believed in them. After not being a star student in grade school or high school, my family was surprised when I announced I was going to college. I never thought it was an option *not* to attend college. I had a plan, and college was part of that plan. My childhood friend reminded me, when I called to wish her a happy birthday, that my plans started when we were teenagers. I was excited to learn during the call that she was going back to school for medical billing. "Thank you," she replied, "I just wish I would have taken you more seriously when you used to ask me what my five-year plan was."

I graduated college, but it didn't come without a challenge and a little innovation. I recall in my senior year asking my counselor what I could do to graduate without going back into a classroom. Mentally, I did not want to struggle through course work that required reading. Lucky for me, my counselor assigned me a 75-page paper and an intro to flowers class. If I successfully completed them both, I'd be out of there!

Needless to say, I successfully completed both the paper and the intro to flowers class. Speaking of flowers, I'd like to send my college counselor flowers as well. Had she not tailored a curriculum that fit my needs, I may be sharing a different story right now!

I understand now that ADD and ADHD is prevalent in our society and hits hard. With a classroom of kids who learn in different ways, how can the schools ensure everyone is learning the way their mind was designed to? That's another book, but for those of you parents who see your children struggling, do your research, and talk to the teachers. For you adults, find ways to manage it. ADD is simply part of who you are and you just need to learn how to live with it. It's part of your design, and can help you in situations rather than hold you back.

Even though I received enough support to allow me to make it through school, I wish my kryptonite had been identified earlier in life; that way I could have worked on how to use it, control it, and manage it. ADD is part of the person I am today and has been a contributing factor to my well thought-out and organized daily routine. As a matter of fact, ADD was a major part of the way I functioned even before I knew I had it.

Let me share with you how I discovered my ADD. I have a love for self-help and business books. One day, I purchased three best-selling self-help books I'd heard great reviews about in my network. Although I struggled to read the books—to the point where I actually didn't complete any of them—I was great at reading the first and last sentence of each paragraph. From there, I filled in the blanks with my own imagination.

I had already realized earlier in life that my conversations were all over the place and I could barely focus on one thing at a time. But it was reading the books, or attempting to read the books, that made me start analyzing myself.

Within a year of recognizing this was an issue for me, I attended a conference required by my job at the time. The guest speaker opened up the meeting by saying, "I'm setting a timer, and after every five minutes of my presentation, I want you to stand up and then sit back down." He explained his reason for this exercise was because of the high percentage of sales representatives having ADD, and this was the only way to ensure he had our undivided attention for his thirty-minute presentation.

Next, he asked us to raise our hand if we could read a page in a book, and at the end, barely remember what we'd just read. I'm not sure who raised their hands, because I didn't look around. I was too shocked that someone understood what I was going through. Had this guy been there solely for me? Was he the answer to the questions I had floating in my mind about why my attention span always seemed to fail me?

By the time his work-related presentation was over, he'd practically diagnosed my life-related issues, AKA my kryptonite. It took me a while to figure out how to use my ADD for good, but what started out as a hindrance and a curse, I now looked at as a gift and one of my superpowers. I have the ability to hyper focus. It may not be when I want to or on what I should be focused on, but as long as I understand that I'm able to adjust my schedule for when I have the hyper focused burst, it works in my favor.

When you begin to recognize your own gifts, you set the stage for real world success. But there are always going to be obstacles that come before you. Identifying them is step one. Is it a person? A place or thing? Multiple things? Once you identify them, you can fight against them.

Next, you have to accept your weaknesses, and just like I did, use them in your favor (Talk about if you can't beat 'em, join 'em!). But whatever you do, don't use weaknesses as an excuse to fail.

Once you realize you need to fight against your kryptonite, you can execute your plan to take action. But simply knowing your abilities (or what some may look at as disabilities or inabilities) changes everything.

I work with ADD and not allow it to work against me by doing the following:

-I set multiple alarms throughout the day to remind me of something I need to do.

-I try not to overload my calendar, because my mind will fill it in when I'm off thinking about something else.

-I have mastered organizational skills to assist me.

-I keep a notebook close by or use my notes app on my phone to clear my mind.

Five things that you can do when it comes to the kryptonite in your life:

1. Identify the kryptonite (person, place or thing).

2. Accept the kryptonite (don't ignore it; face it head on).

3. Release it or use it.

4. Don't worry about what others think.

5. Take action (learn to use it in your favor; as a gift/superpower; don't let it control you).

Taking action may include many things. If a

person is your kryptonite, forgiveness may be involved. Don't exclude yourself. It's possible that you could, in fact, be your own kryptonite, which will cause for self-forgiveness.

Taking action may be challenging if it's a certain obstacle you must overcome. Fear is paralyzing and is probably one of the most familiar forms of kryptonite. What are some of your fears? What are ways you can overcome them (and don't be embarrassed to use Nike's slogan either—Just do it!)? What steps are you willing to take to overcome your fears?

Kryptonite can hold you back and or make you powerless just like it does with Superman, but notice that Superman always manages to fight through it. So can you! ADD is now one of my superpowers, and because of it, I can do things others can't. Look at the irony in that: Your Kryptonite can actually be your superpower!

CHAPTER 6
RETURN TO LOVE

When it comes to Obi Wan Kenobi, most may refer to him more so as a super Jedi versus a superhero. Jedis are self-aware, compassionate, intuitive, overly patient people who prioritize meditating and caution against fear consuming oneself. So, when it comes to stating what Obi's superpower is, take your pick. There's Obi's connection to the universe, his intuition, his patience, his compassion, his selflessness, and his love. Sounds more like human traits and characteristics than superpowers, right? If I had to sum up Obi in one word, it would most definitely be love. Not romantic love, but the unconditional love most of us feel and have for our parents and children, or the kind of love we understand God to have for all living things.

One of my favorite books is about love. It's titled *Return to Love* by Marianne Williamson. In the book, Marianne states that love is kindness, acceptance, non-judgement, giving, mercy, compassion, peace, joy, and a couple other characteristics that you don't have to be a superhero to possess. Love is one of the easiest choices we as humans can make in every situation.

Can you imagine a world where people actually consider love prior to speaking to or engaging someone negatively? I find myself saying, "Think with love today" or "Put love first today." This thought process doesn't apply only to my friends and family. It goes into the world with me when I get cut off on the road, when someone races in front of me to get in line first, and when a business counterpart does or says something rude. In the back of my mind, I'm saying to myself, "Speak with love. React with love." It actually works and reduces the anxiety that would normally build up. This takes daily practice, because there are definitely times when I want to just give it to them. "Remember to think with love," I tell myself.

It's a choice to see the good in our loved ones and people in general. If you see the good in someone, then your response to them will be different even if you feel attacked. Love allows you to focus on the positive and not the negative. We can learn a lot from Obi. He can remind us that it's not always about us. Remembering to love is a great choice. Remembering to love is easy, because we are born with love and have an endless amount of it. Dr. Maya Angelou said, "Love liberates, it doesn't just hold . . . love liberates."

When we embrace love, it's a connection to who we are meant to be. Choosing to love is easier than choosing to hate. Choosing to love comes with great return. You'll get love back in so many ways. If I give you respect, encouragement, and believe in you, it doesn't matter if you give it back to me or not. It will come back to me through other means. I'm confident I will experience love in abundance and so will you. We can't always wait for others to show us love and kindness. Sometimes we have to lead. If we can lead and master it, perhaps so can those who are watching us as an example.

Speaking of mastering, Obi Wan Kenobi is a Jedi Master on the council. His master was Qui Gon Gin and his apprentice was Anakin Skywalker, who we all would become to know as Darth Vader. Notice Obi's tribe consisted of someone who was his teacher, and someone who was the student. Knowing when to lead and when to follow is a crucial part of growing as a person and excelling into "expert" status in your industry.

Known as 'the great negotiator,' Obi always tends to be the most patient and level-headed person in any situation. The way I described Obi seems like he's pretty near perfect, right? The epitome of the fruits of the spirit? He's all that being human entails, yet flawless in his demeanor and character. But is it possible that because Obi is governed by dogma—old ways of thinking—that it often prevents him from doing what it takes to . . . I don't know . . . push forward, perhaps? Be more than what he already is? Reach for higher levels of greatness? Or does he settle there?

I know some of you are probably saying, "He's darn near perfect. That's good enough!" But is 'good enough' really good enough if it can be better? Can 'better' be good enough if it's not your best? Can better be good enough if you haven't reached your true potential? No, I'm not trying to put the pressure on you or anything like that. Of course, we aren't near perfect like Obi, but we should strive to be.

Think of the last task you completed. Maybe, like myself, it was publishing a book. Was there a step in the process you decided to skim on or skip altogether, using the rationalization of, "It's good

Discover Your Superpowers

enough?" But what if it could have served someone else better? What if it was 'good enough' for you, but could have made the difference between life and death for someone else?

Okay, so maybe that's going a little overboard. But just imagine if every time we set out to do something, especially if it could benefit someone else, we treated it as a matter of life and death. You don't let fear or ego take over your decision-making; you put 100% of your efforts into your goals and vision for yourself and others. Seems like an easy enough task, but often, subconscious fears and beliefs based on past trauma or experiences cloud your decision-making and alter your vision, allowing you to justify the 'it's good enough' mentality.

Life is a roadmap of decision-making. Sometimes you only get one try. Sometimes you are put in a situation where you are forced to make decisions; situations where the decision-making process solely lies on you. If you haven't figured it out by now, life is a path of decision-making. What do you do when you're in a tough spot and have to make a decision?

I was taught at a young age to make good decisions. I was instructed to make a list of the pros and cons of the decision that was being contemplated. I was then asked to determine if the pros outweighed the cons. I was also taught to think about the outcome. If I decide to drive without insurance, what would be the outcome if I got stopped by the police? Attorney expenses, court costs, and possibly losing my license. Is it worth not having insurance?

When doing homework, if I wasn't 100% certain about an answer, I had two options; I could either guess and risk putting the wrong answer, or I could spend time doing further research in hopes of finding the correct answer. Doing the latter, I determined, may have been more time consuming, and there was a chance that I still may not find the correct answer, but at least I'd be equipped to make an educated guess if, in fact, it boiled down to such.

My favorite decision-making technique is to base my decision off of the outcome I want. This is why I use a vision board where the desired outcome is posted, and I work backward to achieve the goal.

There is never an excuse to half do anything in life. There is never an excuse to not be and do any and everything you want to do and be in life. And we should never use time or money as a reason why we can't do our best. The universe is full of resources! You have no excuse.

During your "no excuse" journey, you must accept the fact that our life is mapped out. You are here for a reason. Millions of decisions have been made to actually end up with you. Yes, you were born for a reason. Each challenge that comes your way is a learning experience to equip you with the tools and tenacity you need to live and maintain your best life. The sooner you unlock the superhero in you, the sooner you identify your superpowers—what makes you your best (even better than others in certain areas) and those things you can do naturally and seamlessly—then the sooner you can reach your true potential of greatness.

CHAPTER 7
MEDITATION

"Only the strong survive." Cliché or mantra? You can decide for yourself, but however you may interpret the phrase, society has been convinced of the validity of this statement. I will agree that one must be strong in order to break through certain challenges in life, but surviving them—well, that depends on whether one wants to claim the state of surviving, or if one wishes to advance to a state of thriving.

For me, surviving means that you may have made it through something, but you are not necessarily making it through in the after math. You're not thriving after having endured certain circumstances, but merely enduring, remaining, existing.

When dealing with the subject matter of strength, what better superhero to introduce than the Incredible Hulk? He is equipped with not just strength, but brute strength. Bruce Banner, who has his doctorate in nuclear physics, was supervising the trial of an experimental gamma bomb that he'd designed himself. During this time, he witnessed a civilian wander into the testing area. Bruce rushed to save him as an explosion took place. Bruce survived the explosion, but as a result of him playing . . . well . . . a superhero, he experienced extremely high levels of radiation from the gamma bomb.

Ever found yourself in a trying situation all because you were trying to help someone else out? Talk about no good deed goes unpunished . . .

Bruce's condition was successfully treated, with one major side effect; his adrenal medulla secretes large amounts of adrenaline in time of fear, rage, or stress. It's normal for human beings to experience an adrenaline rush during these certain emotional phases, but for Bruce, it's that times 100! So, when you hear someone say, "She went from zero to one-hundred in point five seconds," that sort of the emotional transformation they are referring to is similar to what Bruce experiences.

Just imagine always "going off" to the point

you can't control yourself whenever you are put in situations that are frustrating. If someone says the wrong thing, does the wrong thing, doesn't do something or something doesn't go as planned, you can "pop off" any minute. Try as you might to have some control over your actions, and as many times as you apologize to those affected by your behavior, once again, you "lose it." Perhaps this isn't in your nature at all, but do you know someone who when "once they get started," they can clear a room with their wrath?

Most of the time we excuse such behaviors with "That's just how they are." Often, we even steer clear of people like that, claiming we don't want their bad energy to contaminate our environment. But what if, like Bruce, they simply cannot control it? How do we meet people like that where they are in life? Or do we leave them right where they are, and move on with our own life?

I read on www.superhereodb.com that there were instances in which Bruce became the Hulk without any discernible increase in heart rate or adrenal levels, suggesting that the true trigger mechanism into the Hulk is far more psychological than physical. In regard to Daredevil I asked, "What's in your stomach?" But in this case: "What's in your head?"

Are some people just flat-out mean? Absolutely! But on the same token, some people have psychological reasons beyond their control that cause them to tick. The thing is, they struggle with their behavior internally as much as those around them struggle with it externally. Unfortunately, some may be dealing with undiagnosed bi-polar disorder or other physiological issues the same way I went years not realizing I had ADD.

Bruce has an inability to control his emotion of anger. Do you find yourself feeling as though there are occasions when you experience that same, for lack of a better term, superpower? Not sounding so much like a superpower one would desire to be known for, huh? So why would you want to be known for it by your peers, tribe or community? You wouldn't, I might safely assume.

Certainly you've heard the term "raging." It's defined as one showing violent, uncontrollable anger. The main power Bruce has is strength, and it happens to be a power that he has absolutely no control over, and, ironically, it derives from him not having control over his anger.

Strength will only get Bruce so far. In addition to great strength, the Hulk's body possesses a high degree of resistance to injury. Imagine someone using their emotions of anger as something to keep them from being hurt.

We try to be strong and tenacious and hold our head high, but we are meant to be multidimensional and have compassion for ourselves and others. We should be able to apply reason/logic and be vulnerable with ourselves and others.

I'd like to discuss the missing level of emotions we choose often not to discuss: fear, anxiety, insecurity, uncertainty, feeling threatened, feeling wronged, rejection, sadness, loneliness, vulnerability, disappointment, and shame.

Do you recall being told to "stay in a child's place?" Or if hurt—body or feelings—being told to stop crying? I'd assume most of my generation was taught this so-called "coping mechanism," and, unfortunately, some of us got caught up in this generational curse of not letting emotions show . . . even passing it on to our own children.

It's hard for people to identity the emotions before rage or anger, so we are a walking generation of angry people with pent up emotions. Understanding this level of emotions and being able to identify them will help with our lack of communication.

Picture a conversation with a spouse or friend in which you are able to share your feelings of fear instead of attacking them for something they did. You might be afraid to lose a friendship or marriage, but still, you have a hard time tapping into your emotions to share.

Emotions that fester, are pent up, or suppressed can be detrimental. Learning how to handle negative emotions is a way to ensure you're on track to reach your true potential.

My business partner and cousin, Manika, can probably relate more than anybody I know to not having control of one's emotions. For Manika, not addressing her anxiety, insecurity, disappointment, sadness, and depression got the best of her life. Eventually, though, she was able to conquer her depression with acceptance and meditation.

For Manika, anxiety and depression came like a thief in the night, slowly taking from her what could be considered the most precious thing in life; her ability to be present in each moment. She slowly lost interest in things that once excited her. It was as if the life was being sucked out of her. Her energy level seemed to be depleting on a daily basis. Most people think that depression is due to a lack of happiness, but in all actuality, depression is in spite of happiness.

If I were a copywriter and had to come up with a blurb for the anxiety and depression, it would be: "Depression and anxiety; the double-edged sword." There is the depression, which can take a person to an emotional all-time low. A person suffering from depression may, in the moment, wish for nothing more than to be full of energy. Then along comes anxiety, the other end of the spectrum that can cause worry, nervousness, unease, angst, and agitation, making one feel as if their insides are about to explode. The irony of suffering from both anxiety and depression is that one may find themselves depressed about their past, yet deal with anxiety about the future.

Manika suffered from a bout of post-partum depression. It wasn't until she had a mini-meltdown that she went to her physician, who then prescribed the big "M"; medication. But it was the bigger "M" he suggested that did the trick for Manika's condition; meditation. The Yoga Nidra audio tape saved her life . . . and her mind.

After a month of both medication and meditation, Manika realized the medication was chemically suppressing her emotions and tears, meaning she still felt bad deep down, but no longer expressed it physically. Fortunately, meditation was healing her soul, so she felt naturally good after mediation, and wanted more natural highs. She began researching other things to help her mentally, things that weren't common in her culture; things such as mindfulness meditation, sound meditation, yoga, human design, and life coaching. Through these sources, she began to recognize her limiting beliefs about herself and capabilities.

She realized that her curse was really a gift unique to her. She began to use her feelings as a GPS for her sanity. She enjoyed the challenge of figuring out why she was beginning to feel bad or anxious. Was it a fear that needed to be checked? Was it a challenge that needed to be conquered? Or was it an opportunity not aligned with her goals?

She no longer looked at anxiety and depression as a negative label, but instead, as something that incited her to dissect her inner being for understanding. This allowed her to see it from a positive perspective. She used it to help recognize her superpowers came from a place of vulnerability and sensitivity. Her sensitivity allowed her to empathize and help others. It also allowed her to learn how to follow her gut and redirect her course when something didn't feel right.

I've gone to a few counselors in my life. The one who stands out the most told me to raise my hand and say, "I'm having a feeling." It's okay to acknowledge, or in my case announce, what you are feeling. Adults can be some of the most emotional people, and it's because they haven't been taught how to identify the emotion they are experiencing, understand they're having one, accept it, and talk about it. Since when is it cool to talk about a fear or insecurity you may be having?

Nobody wants to admit they are afraid, ashamed, sad, discouraged, embarrassed, disappointed or confused. But if we could identify the emotion, understand where it's coming from and discuss it, that would change our lives.

The reason I wanted to discuss emotions in this chapter in detail is because we all have them. Do you use your emotions for good or bad? Are your emotions a strength (superpower) or a weakness (kryptonite)? In order to truly understand your superpowers, you need to understand your emotions. In order to propel you to the next level in your life that's filled with opportunity, abundance and pleasantries, you must know who you are intimately.

We discussed mindfulness in chapter three and touched on mediation just a bit, but I would do you a disservice by not digging deeper into meditation and the benefits. Simply breathing deeply has such value. The purpose of meditation is to help your mind feel calm and peaceful; clear your thoughts, and remove the voices.

Meditation creates a space to allow us to control

our minds. With the hectic schedules and demands of modern life, we must incorporate something to help cope. The stress and lack of energy can make you feel unhappy, frustrated, and grumpy. Meditation can take you from a negative to a positive mindset in just 10 minutes. It can take you from feeling unhappy to happy in 10 minutes. In 10 minutes, it can take you from feeling overwhelmed to feeling like you have plenty of time to complete your task.

Meditation is not easy. It takes practice . . . lots of it. Our minds have been wandering for years, and to quiet a mind takes effort and practice. If initially you find it difficult to focus, don't get discouraged. There are lots of postures, ways to breathe, and guided mediation. Find what feels good to you and remember you can do this for five to ten minutes a day to make a difference in your life.

If you find your mind going in the direction it's been going your entire life, just bring it back to your breath, the music you're listening to, or back to the quietness in your mind. The goal is to not think about anything. Yes, it's not easy, but don't give up. The more you bring your mind back to the focal point, the more it will learn to stay in that space of peace. The more you practice, the less you'll find yourself having to draw your mind back. Don't give up on this—I can't reiterate that enough. Meditation is life-changing to the point where you can enjoy the rest of your life in peace. It can help with depression, anxiety, eating disorders, panic disorders, self-esteem issues and lots of other things, but most importantly, it can help you reach your true potential with peace of mind.

97

Discover Your Superpowers

CHAPTER 8
MEETING THE EXPECTATIONS AND COMPARING YOURSELF TO OTHERS

*D*id you think a man was the only superhero whose superpower is "everything?" Well, if you did, think again. The world of superheroes is also one of equal opportunity.

Super Girl, like Superman, was also sent to Earth by her parents for her protection. She wasn't a baby like Superman, though. At the age of 11, this preteen was actually sent to protect Superman while he was just an infant at the time. Her ship (transportation) was knocked off its trajectory, and she didn't make it to earth until Superman was an adult; well into his career as a reporter. It just so happens that she stayed frozen in her ship and was still only 11 years old when she landed on planet

Earth.

It's probably difficult to not be somewhat envious of a chick who has the power to do any and everything. But Super Girl didn't arrive on earth using #girlpower. She hid her powers until one day her adopted sister was on a plane that had engine failure, and she saved the plane.

Do you have skills and know-how that you keep under wraps? Because, after all, once someone knows you are capable of something, they have expectations of you. If you are capable of saving the world, then people will expect you to . . . well . . . save the world. Who wants to live up to those kinds of expectations?!

Believe it or not, some people will keep their abilities hidden in order to avoid expectations and accountability. I'm not sure that was the case with Super Girl, but I know a person or two who could be a millionaire right now if they could only overcome the fear of expectations, accountability, and perhaps the fear of failure.

Do you embrace all of your skills, gifts, talents, and abilities? Or are you afraid that if people knew you could do practically everything, they'd ask, expect, and hold you accountable for everything? Okay, everything is a stretch, but what are you holding back and why?

Are you holding back because you don't want to have to meet the expectations of others? Your needs matter, too, and you shouldn't ignore them. Sometimes you have to do what's best for you and your life, not what others expect you to do.

Did you know that some people are incapable of being pleased? So, whether you meet their expectations or not, they are still going to find somewhere you fall short. Consider the fact that you could be trying to please someone who doesn't have the capacity to be pleased, which means you'll spend your entire life living it for someone else . . . a person who is satisfied with nothing.

I've always looked at it as if I serve myself and not others, I'm giving them a gift, because I will be alive. People around me need me feeling alive, and I'm sure there are people around you who need you alive as well. Your individuality needs to be celebrated, and living your truth and doing what makes you feel alive is worth celebrating. In the end, happiness is simply living life the way *you* want. It's living your best life.

It's not bad for others to have expectations of you, but what is unhealthy is for you to struggle trying to meet the expectations of others. Everyone has a unique gift or talent. I've had two professions in my lifetime. They were the temporary industry days and the pharmaceutical days. While in the temporary industry, I met a gentleman named Bruce who made such a great impact in my life. When I decided to leave the pharmaceutical industry, I shared my decision with Bruce and another manager. I told them I was leaving the industry, moving back to the small town I grew up in, and going to work for the Social Security office. This was something my family thought was best for me, because a government job meant security and having me back in my hometown. I'm sure it was a level of comfort for myself as well.

I gave my two-week notice and had my 30-day notice to vacate the premises all typed up and ready to deliver to my apartment management. Before I was able to do the latter, Bruce sat me down and asked me a very serious question: "What are you thinking?" He went on to tell me how talented I was in sales and recruiting, and how it would be a shame for me to waste my talents with the Social Security office.

Wow! That was such a huge compliment for my young, impressionable self, who was trying to please everybody but myself. How could I have gotten in such a predicament? Imagine being in a situation where you are making a decision based on what others want and not what you want. Or

Discover Your Superpowers

maybe you don't have to imagine, because you've actually been there yourself.

Bruce offered me a job doing 100% outside sales, paying me more money than I would make at the Social Security office. Whether or not to accept his offer was one of the hardest decisions I ever had to make, because I don't like to go against what people expect of me, and my family was expecting me to return home. Bruce expected me to stay with the company. I was such a people pleaser at the time, making the decision more difficult than ever.

This was an opportunity for me to go on a path to find my purpose and passion, because I definitely knew the Social Security office couldn't offer me that. Purpose and passion can change as you gain additional knowledge, skills, and experience. My passion has changed over the years, but it's always loosely been revolved around helping people.

Today, my purpose and passion is to make a difference in others' lives using this book as a vehicle to do so. When someone tells me that this book changed their life, then I will feel confident that part of my destiny has been fulfilled. That's when I can finally say I'm walking in my purpose and passion, and I will then feel I've achieved what success means to me.

And by the way: heck yeah, I took Bruce up on his offer! When a path is made that can lead you to your passion and purpose, don't be afraid to take it. It doesn't always necessarily have to be the road less traveled, but instead, a road that has already been paved just for you!

In a sense, Superman paved the way for Super Girl. Once word got out about Super Girl's powers, she decided to embrace being a superhero. In spite of all that Super Girl is capable of doing, her 'everything' is often compared to Superman's 'everything'. So, to show that she's just as capable and able as her counterpart, Super Girl places herself on certain missions, refusing to ask for help. After all, Superman didn't ask for any help.

This tactic sometimes puts Super Girl in compromising situations. How many times have you compromised yourself, others, your career, and your success simply because you didn't seek help? You didn't want people to think you were weak?

For the sake of this book, it sounds like Super Girl's kryptonite could be comparing herself to others. So what Superman has been leaping tall buildings in a single bound longer than her. He's seasoned, while Super Girl was planted on Earth much later. So, like the saying goes, Super

Girl should not compare her planting season to Superman's harvest season.

How many times have you looked at someone who does exactly what you do, but are further along success-wise, and began to doubt yourself? Did you ever stop to think that perhaps that other person has been at this double the amount of time you have? That what looks like their overnight success took over a decade? But who cares about where they are in life? Even if you started at the same place and same time as your competitor, wherever you are on your journey isn't about anyone else (or <u>because</u> of anyone else . . . no playing the blame game). This is where you have to trust the process. Trust that if someone is excelling more in one area, that you are excelling in another area that matters more to you than that person. Trust that you are where you're supposed to be, and that you will end up exactly where you are supposed to.

Discover Your Superpowers

CHAPTER 9
FEAR AND EXCUSES

With all the talk about STEM, or as some now refer to it, STEAM, Ironman is like a technology engineering superhero. Not only that, but when he's not in Iron Man mode, Tony Stark is an extremely smart, fast-talking playboy who inherited his father's empire, Stark Industries, when his parents were killed in a car accident.

Tony Stark can be considered a self-proclaimed superhero. After all, he did create that entire Iron Man getup, which he personally brings to life. The special suit gives him superhuman abilities and strengths, and the suit is equipped with powerful weapons. So, would you say it's Tony Stark that makes Iron Man the superhero, or the Iron Man that makes Tony Stark a superhero? I'm thinking that perhaps they simply complement one another.

Oddly enough, Tony Stark doesn't have any superpowers at all, yet he's considered a superhero because he was smart enough to build one (giving new meaning to the term 'self-made'). One can say Iron Man's superpower is the man behind the genius mind; the creator, AKA Tony Stark. At the same time, Iron Man's weakness is the man behind the creation of Iron Man. Oh, the irony of it all!

Tony's ego often appears to be much larger than what the suit can handle. His need to always be right, along with his stubbornness and selfish attitude, are major setbacks in him being able to achieve more. Ever felt like you had the ability to do anything you put your mind to, but then along came your worst enemy to hinder you—yourself?

What are some of the thoughts you've had, things you've said, or things you've done that have gotten in the way of you accomplishing something or excelling in an area? Remember, this isn't about what you feel or think someone else has taken part in. It's all about you. After all, isn't that how the ego prefers it?

There are so many times in life where I was so close to reaching my dreams and goals. I was working hard, doing everything I possibly could to make things happen, but it always felt like something was getting in my way. For quite some time I couldn't figure out what it was, then one day I looked in the mirror, and there it was; me. I was getting in my own way.

Can you think of times when things just didn't seem as if they were taking off, then you realized that it was because of you? It was because of your excuses and self-doubt? Life isn't about excuses, but instead, about how you can persevere through life. You are responsible for you.

Some things in life require a little self-discipline (or a lot). One thing I know for sure in my life that requires discipline is me . . . when I'm by myself. Once you can stand to be alone in the same room with yourself, then you're headed toward self-acceptance, awareness, and appreciation. There's no one there for the ego to impress. You no longer find yourself pulling on others to make you feel happy, accomplished, or successful.

According to Wikipedia, egotism is the drive to maintain and enhance favorable views of oneself, and generally features an inflated opinion of one's personal features and importance. It often includes intellectual, physical, social, and other overestimations. Do you or anyone you know sometimes fit that description when around others? Do you know that person who is so full of helium you can see them about to explode?

Most of the time, the reason why people need to feel like the biggest person in the room is because they actually feel like the smallest. Just think about it, when you're alone, you actually are the biggest person in the room. Of course, it's because you're the *only* person in the room. But again, if you can apply the necessary self-discipline to be okay with you, who you are, what you are, and where you are in life, then others won't have to be subjected to your efforts of you shrinking them. In my perfect world, we're all equal, and there is nothing I love more than being in a room full of giants!

Tony's suit makes him feel like the big man on campus. Unfortunately for him, being in a room alone may not be the antidote to cure his egotism. Did you know that Tony Stark can never be separated from his creation? His suit has the ability to store itself inside Tony's bones. It meshes with his body and mind. What are you hiding inside of you? What's meshing with your body and mind that you don't want to separate yourself from?

Tony is always on. In life, you have to know when to turn it on, and when to turn it off . . . or sometimes when to just tune it down a little bit. But because he can't separate himself from his suit— his creation—he can't simply turn it off. What suit have you clad yourself in? One that seems to run deep in your bones?

Mine is fear. Yep, I created it and refused to separate myself from it. Do you think that's why Tony made it so that he can't separate himself from his suit? He's afraid? Afraid that the "brand" he created is not really who he is, and that he'll be found out?

Having fear-based thoughts can be detrimental to anyone with a destiny to reach, and a purpose to fulfill. If you don't try something, then you've already failed. I'm going to say that in another way to make sure you get the message. That thing (goal or task) you have in your head—the one you've always wanted to do but haven't, because you don't want to fail—you have already failed at it, because you haven't even tried to accomplish it.

In my younger days, I was fearless! I tried my hand at multiple businesses with no fear, but as an adult, my passion and purpose business comes with lots of fear. You're reading this book because I managed to get past one of my fears.

I've always told myself that I was going to write down a list of all the businesses I've attempted throughout my life, so here it goes:

1. Does the Easy Bake Oven cake sales with

Becky Brooks in the 5th grade count?

2. Selling Now and Laters out of my locker in the seventh grade has to count.

3. Producing and selling an all-female calendar in college

4. Sold an oxygen bar into one of the largest amusement parks in the country and managed it with Nena and Jason

5. Multilevel marketing company #1 with Tiana

6. State purchasing company with Nannette

7. Fat burning machine

8. Spa consultant

9. Vitamin deficiency device with Nicole

10. Multilevel marketing #2 with Manika

11. T&S Aesthetics with Staci

12. Rep Network (current company)

13. Aesthetics by Design (current company)

14. The1 (sold)

15. Rental company with my husband

16. Your True Potential with Manika and Dr. Kee

I'm sure I'm missing a few.

The reason I wanted to put this list together is to demonstrate that in the past, I went after what I wanted in business without any fear. But the one business that is actually tied into my passion and purpose I have put off until now. I've known I wanted to write a book since I was a teenager, but with my ADD and past school experience, I was afraid it was something I wasn't going to be able to accomplish. I am attempting to master the skills to be a phenomenal superhero, and getting past fears is my challenge.

I have this message, right? But with a message comes great responsibility. That responsibility has always given me great fear. My fear goes deeper than just the responsibility. I have never felt old enough to put a message out, wise enough, talented enough, or successful enough. So, when I figured out that it was my time to do this, it didn't come without fear. But I refused to let fear hold me back. I refused to be in my own way.

Just because I'm actually putting my thoughts on paper doesn't mean I don't have more fears to overcome. I created a suit of fear to protect me. I actually don't like to admit this, and I get stomach pains when I think about it, but I'm terribly shy. And here I am writing a book. I refuse to continue to hold back these messages inside of me.

My husband is the one who's challenging me to conquer this fear that he knows has nothing to do with who I truly am. I know that with writing this book comes expectations of me that will require me to overcome this fear, and I WILL do it. Why? Because I'm putting my superpowers to use. I am on track to becoming a phenomenal superhero, leaving my suit of fear behind. Without Ironman's suit he will be the man who created the suit just like Thor and his hammer, but in all reality, they are

capable of being super without the suit and prop. Whatever suit you created to protect yourself, it's time to take it off. You will be extraordinary without it.

I've had to overcome the fear of this, that or the other several times in life. If fear has you bound, I challenge you to push through it. Fear is the cheapest room in the house. I'd like to see you in better living conditions. We've already discussed preparation in an earlier chapter, but to make the connection with this chapter, know that when it comes to reaching your dreams and goals, your fear will not be as great if you're prepared.

Let's not ignore the word 'excuses' and how excuses can be part of the reason you are in your own way. Oh, I had lots of excuses as to why I couldn't move forward with my purpose and passion. I listed some above. Is there actually such a thing as a good excuse? Because, let's face it, they all sound good when we're reciting them. Excuses such as, "the timing isn't right," "the money isn't right" (not enough), "I need more education," I need a partner," etc. To answer the question: "No!" There is never a good excuse not to fulfill your purpose and passion. There is never a good excuse as to why you can't reach your true potential. But if you need some additional time to "prepare" yourself, then that's okay. Preparation is not an excuse . . . procrastination is. Don't mix up the two.

Preparation is what must greet opportunity at the door. What doors of opportunity are you waiting to open up for you? Are you prepared once opportunity does presents itself?

If the timing isn't right, what will make it right and what do you need to do in order to prepare yourself for when the timing is right? As a matter of fact, define exactly what the right timing is.

I'm waiting . . .

Thought so.

What are you waiting for? Let's accept that whole "right timing" thing for what it is; an excuse. And as far as money, if you need to save more money, are you? How, and are you researching and positioning yourself to get more of it? Do you have a second job or what I call "a side hustle?" We spend what we make, so make more (legally, of course)!

If you need more education, then get it. The web has every course imaginable. Heck, on a good day, so does Groupon! Do your due diligence and you'll find some very affordable educational courses . . . some are even free.

If your excuse is not knowing what your passion or your purpose is, then go back to the basics of what I said in an earlier chapter: "Shut up and listen." What puts a smile on your face during your quiet time? More than likely, it will be the same thing that puts a smile on your face when experiencing the noise of the world. And ironically, it will be the same thing that helps you silence the noise around you, while you contribute that gift inside of you . . . to the world.

CHAPTER 10
CIRCULATION OF GIVING AND RECEIVING

Like some of the superheroes we've discussed, Spiderman has quite a few superpowers, but the one I'd like to focus on for the sake of this chapter is his ability to give unconditionally. Sure, it's pretty impressive that he is fifteen times more agile than a human and has superhuman strength, but the fact that simply out of the kindness of his heart he can sense, prepare for, and act accordingly to something before it causes harm or does serious damage is matchless.

Before turning into Spiderman, Peter Parker was bitten on the hand by a radioactive spider. Radioactive mutagenic enzymes in the spider's venom empowered Peter with the arachnid's proportional strength and agility as well as the ability to cling to almost any surface.

Sure, we call him Spiderman, but hey, Peter's just a kid. Imagine what it must feel like to be underestimated just because you are younger than your peers. Society doesn't expect or believe a person is able or capable of doing certain things unless they've reached a certain age in life. It brings to mind a conversation my editor and friend, Joylynn Ross, had with her daughter. She asked her daughter what she wanted to be when she grew up, and her daughter's response was, "Why do I have to wait until I grow up? Why can't I be it now?"

It's good to have that childlike reliance that allows you to dream and imagine big. It allows you to see the good in people and treat people equally regardless of what you've been told by others, giving them their fair chance. As adults, whether it's in the workplace or doing a good deed, we often seek some type of recognition or reward. Young Peter helps others and does good deeds even if he doesn't get credit for them.

The newspapers often question his motives, and some people think he is a vigilante or causes too many problems for the city. Of course, he struggles with the opinions others have of him. But at the end of the day, he knows what his intentions are.

What are your intentions in life?

Why do you do some of the things you do (good or bad)? What are you seeking within, (if you're seeking anything at all)?

I admire Spiderman because he's a giver and never expects anything back. We should all have the best of intentions in everything we do in life . . . regardless of who is watching or paying attention, or if we'll get credit for it. Sounds a great deal like the definition of integrity.

Did you know there is actually a law that Deepak Chopra shed conscious light on called "The Law of Giving and Receiving?" It's the second law in his book, *The 7 Spiritual Laws of Success*. Deepak says we must give and receive in order to keep money, or anything we want, circulating in our lives.

Your giving must be intentional.

The circulation of giving and receiving is what keeps the world going around and us all alive. I know people who feel like they have to hold onto their money for the sake of not receiving more. The act of giving must feel good to you and be genuine in order to circulate back to you.

I have a funny story I'd like to share with you. One winter, I took my children downtown with a friend to pass out blankets to the homeless. We drove around looking for people who needed blankets, scarves, and gloves. At the end of one evening, we unloaded the car at the men's shelter prior to going home. My friend and I had smiles on our faces from the feeling of giving. My oldest son and my friend's son were around seven at the time, and my youngest son was four. I was video recording the three kids, and asking questions about the evening and how it made them feel to do something so nice. My four-year-old spoke up and said, "Well I'm a little sad."

I instantly stopped the recording, because I had no clue what he was about to say. I knew he had the potential to ruin the video. I went on to ask him why he was sad and he replied, "I gave that guy my last blanket, and now I'm a little cold."

If he wasn't four years old, I would have been mortified. But because he was four, it was super funny to all of us. But needless to say, he blocked the circulation of giving and receiving that evening by not giving unconditionally and from the heart. I'm working on him. But you . . . give from the heart and without expectations or needing recognition. Trust the process and that it'll come back to you.

Those referred to as "givers" tend to give in secret. They don't need the world to know their acts, neither do they have the desire to receive any type of recognition. They give even when they don't have it to give, believing that it will come back to them in some form. If it's respect you're looking for, then give respect and respect will come back to you. Giving and receiving doesn't always need to be monetary. Compliments, time, knowledge, smile, a ride to work, picking up groceries for a single mom, or shoveling snow for an elderly neighbor are all forms of giving.

On a daily basis, I smile at the lady entering the daycare and wave to the FedEx and UPS drivers coming down the street. I compliment people on their outfits. I give larger tips when I hear that it's the waiter's birthday. I send text messages to let people know that I'm thinking about them when they cross my mind.

One time during my son's football game, I noticed a lady struggling with her infant who was probably hot because of the sun. I gave her my umbrella and told her she could use it during the game to help the infant be more comfortable. She was so appreciative. It's just the little things.

I enjoy helping and giving more than anything, because I love the way it makes me feel. (And it doesn't require me announcing to the world on social media or at family gatherings every time I engage in an act of kindness.) When one does this, that's when, like with Spiderman, people may begin to question their intentions. Although that person may mean well and only want to help, allowing the feeling that serving others gives you inside should be the only reward you need. But lucky for you, you will reap the benefits as well.

Whatever you put out comes right back to you, regardless if it's good or bad. Get clear about what you're putting out. You have to set your intentions, and you can start by asking yourself what it is you want to get back from life, then start giving it to receive it.

CHAPTER 11
TURNING BAD INTO GOOD WITH PREPARATION AND TRAINING

*I*n this chapter, I'd like to focus on Batman. I know what you're thinking already: How can someone with no superpowers be a superhero? I get it. As I began to do my research for this book, I thought the same thing. I searched high and low for a resource that may know of Batman's unknown superpowers. Every source I tapped into pretty much reads like this Wikipedia definition: "Unlike most superheroes, Batman does not possess any superpowers; rather, he relies on his genius intellect, physical prowess, martial arts abilities, detective skills, science and technology, vast wealth, intimidation, and indomitable will."

How can Batman be . . . well . . . superpower-less? I mean, he's taken on some of Gotham City's most notorious villains and defeated them! So, who is this Batman, and what on Earth qualifies him as a superhero?

Bruce Wayne was orphaned at a young age when his parents were shot in front of him by a mugger. He spent his youth traveling the world, training himself to intellectual and physical perfection, and learning a variety of crime-fighting skills, including chemistry, criminology, forensics, martial arts, gymnastics, disguise, and escape artistry. It's safe to say that Bruce pretty much trained himself to be super.

Imagine that! When surrounding circumstances show beyond a shadow of a doubt that you are no challenge for life's battles—when people begin to count you out; when resources, time and money are scarce; when it simply doesn't look as though life was cut out for you to win—you still have to prepare yourself for the fight. Even if every ounce of your being believes that you weren't born with anything great inside of you, train yourself for greatness. Prepare to win in spite of your situation looking like a loss.

I'm an optimist, so even though I don't expect the worst in life, I prepare for it. Even if everything around me looks like I'm going to lose, I prepare to win.

Win, lose, or draw, like I mentioned in chapter 9, you've already failed if you don't even try. Lack of preparation is equivalent to throwing in the towel; giving up; showing no future efforts in getting the win.

Preparation requires training. Superheroes are in constant battles, which mean they are always fighting. A fighter requires training. You can't just jump into the ring with Mike Tyson and expect to win. But is it possible for you to win? Absolutely . . . Anything is possible. Just think of how great your chances of winning the fight would be with the proper preparation and training.

Even for those born with natural gifts, talents, and skills, training enhances and sharpens those qualities which already exist. So, if there are some great things you desire to do, then prepare yourself by training yourself to be great in order to achieve them.

When I think of training, my oldest son comes to my mind. He's eight and has been training himself to master his passions since he was four. He loves technology. You're probably thinking that all kids his age love technology, but he takes his love a few steps further. He's the kid who will grab your phone, and next thing you know, Siri is calling you by his name. Or he will tap your Apple watch a few times, and the Avengers is your new screen saver. His favorite outing is to a cellular store. Technology is something he has a passion for and he actually has been self-training himself for years.

Right when I think I'll find him watching a cartoon on his device in his spare time, he'll actually be watching instructional videos on the web about a watch, phone, tablet, game console, or some new technology coming out soon. Because of the training he puts himself through, he can have a conversation about phone drop test with the technology store manager, the features, benefits, and differences of Chromebooks, and can teach the administrative staff at his elementary school how to use their gadgets. Not only does he already know one of his passions, but he's on a mission to master it. When you add passion and training together, your superpowers will ignite.

Now just because you train yourself for greatness doesn't mean there aren't going to be any struggles in life. Regardless of how well-trained Bruce was in certain areas, he had plenty of struggles. One was him not wanting to be part of Wayne Enterprises, an empire built by his father. Even though Bruce inherited Wayne Enterprises, most of the business decisions are made by Lucius Fox, Bruce's business manager. After all, who has time to run a business when they're off trying to save the world?

Allow me to take a pause here for all you entrepreneurs, solopreneurs, and business owners. A business should be able to operate without you. You should be able to stay home in bed when you're sick, go to your children's, grandchildren's or niece's and nephew's events, or go on vacation. There should be more people laying the bricks to your empire than just yourself. Now back to our regularly scheduled program already in progress . . .

Eventually, Bruce swears an oath to rid the city of the evil that took his parents' lives. Superman may be considered the Man of Steel, but Batman has a heart of steel. He would give his life to save just one innocent person. But that's not his measure of success; he wants to save everyone.

What's your measure of success? What is your profession, or hobby? What milestone has to take place for you to deem yourself successful in that area? Batman wants to save everyone. We can start with saving one person at a time, and the first person to save is YOURSELF.

Although Batman is considered to have no

superpowers, he, like his counterparts, has a weakness; his guilt. He is driven by the grief, guilt, and pain of losing his parents and therefore lives in a state of perpetual torment and depression. Sorry, but I have to take another pause.

Here this man is, a superhero, has more money than God, and yet he lives in mental torment and depression. I don't know about you, but I can name at least two or three people who have been functioning like this for years.

Before knowing Batman's backstory, was there something about him that brought you down? Did he come across as kind of drab for a superhero? Now that you know the fact that he functions with grief and depression, do you see him in a different light? Are his characteristics starting to make sense? This just goes to show that you never know someone's story . . . until they tell it. What's your story?

I love a good "happily ever after" story, which is the formula for any great romance novel or Hallmark Channel movie. So, I was intrigued when reading an interview about Author E. N. Joy. She stated that she writes about pain. "We all may never experience a happily ever after in life, but we will all experience pain, and my stories teach you how to operate while in pain, and once you're through it."

Batman allowed grief and loss to drive him. That's true for so many people. But you can't let grief and loss consume you. The most beautiful things come out of adversity, which is the epitome of turning something bad into good. Resilience is key in overcoming life trials. Resolve is the ability to fight through anything and stay focused. What's your resolve? What situation can you look back at and declare, "I made it"?

There is one person in my life who has mastered the art of overcoming grief and pain and turning it into good. She's a true superhero. My friend, Michele, endured what no woman should, and that is burying her young son who committed suicide. This was the most challenging period in her life, because all she wanted to do was pull the covers over her head and go to sleep for the rest of her life; never having to face the world.

After her grieving period, she decided she was going on a mission to prevent others from having to go through what she went through, and to help those suffering from depression. Michele has spent the last few years on a nationwide quest to get physicians to adopt the PGX test, which is a test that allows individuals with unwanted, and at times, deadly, side effects find medicine that would work best for their body. The test provides the knowledge of whether an antidepressant will leave the patient's body sooner than it should. A premature exit from the patient's system means it won't work. On the other hand, if it stays in the body too long, it can cause additional side effects. The ultimate goal is to find the product that stays in the body for the perfect amount of time to ensure the patient is being treated with the best possible medication. Michele has worked tirelessly to get the message out, and has turned something so terrible and tragic into something that can help save many lives.

I recently saw my mother utilize her superpowers when she suffered the loss of her father. It was very painful for her to endure. Of course, losing a parent is never easy. But what I saw from her was immediate action in making sure that his memory was not forgotten. She picked up where he left off in his philanthropy by contributing to his church of choice. She now has a yearly hayride in his name for the kids in the area where he's from, and she attends events in his place that he wouldn't have thought of missing. She's ensuring his memory lives on.

Like it says in the book by Robins Compere, *Embrace Your Life*, whatever it is you must embrace,

do so. Whether it was being abused, neglected, lied to, cheated on, or suffering a loss, embrace it. Then use it to help someone else. Use it to be someone better!

Before I close out this chapter, I want to let you know that I did dig a little further and learned that the video game version of Batman has X-Ray vision. It's referred to as "detective vision." It's part of his suit upgrade projected onto Batman's cowl straight from the Batcomputer. Some of you are probably saying, "That doesn't count." Well, if it counts for Iron Man, then it counts for Batman too!

No, Batman can't do anything super unique like fly, but he can glide his wings off. He can maneuver an aircraft with a maximum speed of 4,400 miles per hour. You try operating something of that magnitude!

I don't know about you, but I consider Batman's genius intellect, which gives him the ability to outsmart his competitors, pretty super. I'm sure if we dig deep enough, we can find many hidden abilities that Batman has that could be considered superpowers, as we could do for every single individual on this earth. This just goes to show that not everyone's gifts, talents, and abilities are immediately recognizable. Sometimes they simply have to be unearthed.

Before reading this chapter, some of you had no idea Batman didn't have superpowers, which ultimately is supposed to qualify someone as a superhero. So now, after reading this chapter (perhaps after reading this book), do you have a different take on what makes someone a superhero? I hope you now have a new outlook on the true definition of a superhero.

CHAPTER 12
FIGHTING FOR A TITLE AND WHAT YOU BELIEVE IN

"Wakanda forever!"

I had to start off this chapter with that. You saw the movie, *Black Panther*. Simply powerful, right? T'Challa, a king and protector of his nation. The heir to the dynasty of the great African kingdom, Wakanda. Wakanda is technologically advanced and full of valuable resources, which they conceal from the outside world. What seems to be the most valuable, yet priceless resource is a meteorite made of vibranium. Wakandans conceal it out of fear that outsiders will exploit Wakanda for its resources.

Wakanda, unlike other nations, was never colonized by Europeans. "Wakanda represents this unbroken chain of achievement of black excellence that never got interrupted by colonialism," Evan Narcisse, a pop culture critic who co-writes "The Rise of the Black Panther" miniseries, told The Washington Post's David Betancourt. Although Wakanda is fictitious, their rubrics don't have to be. It can be a mean world, but the ways of the world don't have to infiltrate your home and the way you do business. As a business owner, you have the power, like T'Challa and those before him, to put systems, rules, and guidelines in place to achieve the living and working conditions that you desire.

Drinking a heart-shaped herb gives Black Panther his superpowers. Along with his proficiency in science, rigorous physical training, hand-to-hand combat skills, and access to wealth and advanced technology, he is able to combat his enemies.

Black Panther is the first superhero of African descent in mainstream American comics. Imagine what it must feel like to be the first, and at least at one point, the only person of your background or nationality to uphold such a title. A trailblazer, for lack of a better term. That's a great deal of weight to carry, yet T'Challa doesn't run away from the challenge, but instead, embraces it . . . fights for it (literally).

Has a great challenge ever been placed before you that you had to fight for? Did you fight or did you bow out gracefully? Did fear of not living up to the expectations of those depending on you (your family, team members, coworkers) cause you to decline?

Black Panther is the title given to the chief of the Panther Tribe in Wakanda. It is a title that is inherited, but at the same time, it must still be earned. Some believe that titles aren't important, and perhaps in certain circumstances they are not. But when one has been tried, tested, and proven they have the abilities to take on a title, then at least to that person, there is great meaning behind it.

What titles have you earned in life? What did you have to go through in order to earn that title? Even if it's being a mother, what did you have to go through? Morning sickness? Months of carrying around excess weight? Hours of labor pains? Months and years of nursing and preparing bottles in the midnight hour? Stretchmarks? What about rising up in a business setting from entry level in fast food or retail? Managing or running your own business, getting a college degree, or being the first in your family to do so? Overcoming anxiety and depression, PTSD, or fear? How about the title of a cancer survivor? When you look at it from this prospective, heck yes, titles are important! Whatever title you may wear, whether it's letters before or after your name, don't allow anyone to devalue it. Think of all you went through to earn that title (Doctor, Esquire, CEO, Father, Coach, Survivor, etc.).

For some, it's not that titles aren't important. As a matter of fact, it can be just the opposite; they can be so important that it causes one to become fearful of seeking out or donning that title. Titles are often connected with a role of authority or leadership. That means others are depending on you because of your title. In T'Challa's case, it was his family and an entire nation who was dependent upon him.

T'Challa had a deep loyalty to his country. Because of that loyalty, he often sacrificed personal interests and relationships, pushing people he cared about away. As leaders, we must understand that the course we are on to fulfill our potential and live a value-aligned lifestyle may mean that some people in our life may not be part of that journey. It is okay to grow apart from loved ones. This is especially true for people pursuing entrepreneurship, moving to another country, or some other 'big' unconventional lifestyle shift that friends and family members may be skeptical or disapproving of because they don't understand (or outright disagree with).

It wasn't until T'Challa developed a brain aneurysm that he separated himself from his family and kingdom. The aneurysm caused him to suffer from hallucinations. When his mental state almost caused tribal warfare, he turned over his power to his council and hid out in New York City. Have you ever had to pass the baton so that you could get your mind right? That's not quitting or giving up—it's doing what's right. Sometimes taking a pause in life is the right thing to do, but don't forget to go back and grab the baton and run with it, just as T'Challa eventually did. While in New York, T'Challa connected with and began to mentor a police officer. This mentorship gave T'Challa the strength to face his illness and reclaim his position.

But let's focus on this mentorship for a moment. Imagine being in a relationship where you believe you are on an assignment to help someone else, yet they end up helping you. Sometimes you are promoted (or even demoted) not only because along that particular journey someone is supposed to meet you, but because you are destined to meet them. Sometimes you have to separate yourself from others (including family) to fulfill part of your destiny.

During the separation process you may feel alone. When problems arise, regardless of how minute they may actually be, because you are alone, you may feel defenseless—already defeated. I say, "Fight, fight, fight, and keep fighting! Fight for your title! Fight for your position! Fight for your destiny!"

Black Panther is able to use a variety of weapons when fighting, but he prefers unarmed combat. He is a master planner who always thinks several steps ahead and will go to extreme measures to achieve his goals. Plan out your battle so that you can win the war.

I enjoy the challenges of fighting for what I believe in and fighting for what I want. Let's just say I've had my fair share of fights along the way to earn specific titles. You know by now I had to fight ADD to get through school and workforce trainings. I had to win that fight to earn the title of not only CEO, but CFO and COO, but don't think for one moment those titles came easy.

I've had to put in 70-hour work weeks to pull it off, ignore phone calls, time with family, etc. I've had to separate myself from people who were in the way, and I've had to remove business partners along the way who ended up being part of the problem and not the solution.

I had to earn the title of being a mother by spending four months in the hospital due to complications. Four months of not being able to sit up except for when eating. Showering every other day, and no sunlight except for a 15-minute visit outside on Thursdays. Labor pains for four months, and the fight of reconnecting after being disconnected. I was this baby's incubator and his best chance for life. I fought for him to have life. The fight didn't stop there. I actually decided to have a second child so the first would have someone to go through this thing called life with. The second time around didn't come without a fight, but I was more prepared and equipped for the challenge. I was educated and mentally prepared for the fight to add another life into the world.

I hold tight to my other titles as well, such as the title of being a wife. I've jumped buildings in a single bound for my husband and everyone who knows me knows how seriously I take my titles in regard to my family. I take my title as a daughter fiercely, and a granddaughter, niece, cousin, as well as friend all seriously. I fight for and treasure all my titles and I encourage you to do the same. No matter how insignificant the title may seem to the rest of the world, it's yours, dang on it! You earned it—it's part of your armor, and it's worth claiming and fighting for.

CHAPTER 13
YOUR SHIELD

There was a time in America when young men were war dodging. The last thing they wanted to do was risk their young lives for a country they'd barely lived in, a country where they hadn't even scratched the surface of all it had to offer. That wasn't the case for Steve Rogers. Steve Rogers desperately wanted to enlist in the military to fight in World War II. Unfortunately, he was rejected due to health issues.

It's not a good feeling when everything in your being—the desires of your heart—is to do this one thing, but for reasons beyond your control, you can't. You want to belong and be a part of something bigger than yourself, but yet you are not accepted. There's something you lack. There's something wrong with you. You keep telling yourself, "I'm not wanted." "I'm not good enough."

No matter how you dice it, and no matter the reasons (legitimate or not), the feeling of rejection is like an injection of imperfection with a great big needle. The side effect is a nauseous feeling of being less than or unwanted. Sometimes in life when we don't get that job, don't make the team, or don't get the girl (or guy), we can hold onto that failure and beat ourselves upside the head with it so much that it becomes embedded in our mental. We can't take hold of something else, something better perhaps, because we're too busy holding onto those lies we tell ourselves.

But for Steve, desperate to reach his dreams by any means necessary, there was a flicker of hope. If his only way of being recruited into the army was by participating in the Strategic Scientific Reserve "super-soldier" experiment, then so be it. How far are you willing to go to reach your dreams? Perhaps there is something you wanted to do—something you wanted to achieve—but you didn't.

Thinking back, were there other means by which you could have achieved it? Maybe the conventional way was out of the question, but perhaps you could have gotten creative and created another route. It's safe to say that Steve's admission into the army was definitely unconventional.

During this experiment, Steve was given a serum that enhanced his physique to human perfection. So as a twist of fate, having once felt like he took in an injection of imperfection, he literally was injected with a dose of perfection. The serum permanently enhanced his strength, durability, and endurance. No more sickliness. The serum was created to aid the United States government's efforts in World War II, so needless to say, Steve was able to live his dream of fighting for his country.

In 1942, close to the end of the war, Steve crashed the plane he was flying into an ocean where he became trapped in ice. And once he thawed out 70 years later, you guessed it, he was alive and still the same age as when he was initially frozen.

Similar to Batman, the superhero Captain America has no superpowers, but what Captain America does have is his shield. Unfortunately, it doesn't seem to have any powers either. No boomerang features or anything of the sort. It is made from vibranium and is indestructible under normal conditions. Even with the greatest of impact, Captain America does not feel recoil or transferred impact forces when using the shield to block attacks.

There was a point where Captain America's shield was attacked by a cancer that damaged the core materials. With the cancer spreading, the shield became a necessary sacrifice in order to save the remaining vibranium, which both directly and indirectly could save the world.

Let's discuss Captain America and his using his shield to block attacks. Do you know what you need to shield yourself against? Perhaps you were in a toxic relationship that threatened to eat up your home and destroy the peace of everyone in it. Perhaps you were in a management position at work and had a toxic employee who was infecting the entire team. Would you be willing to let that person go? Either definitely or indefinitely? Because please note, the shield was eventually restored (cured), and returned to its normal state of strength. Still, there was a period where it had to be sacrificed.

Do you know how to identify what your shield is? What do you have that helps you protect yourself from attacks? Is it your God, the universe, yoga, swimming, serving, sleep, meditation, walking your dog, etc.? I'm going to use yoga as an example of a shield. My friend, who's a yoga instructor, told me that at the end of the practice of yoga, you roll to one side, and that represents being born again. Yoga is her shield. She rolls over and hits the reset button to life. Sure, some may think yoga is pretty trivial. They may even try to damage my friend's shield by stating such, thinking she'll eventually get in agreement. This is a sneaky tactic designed to either damage someone's sword (insert doubt of the effectiveness so that it becomes not so effective), or cause the person to put their sword down (abandon its use altogether).

Has something or someone tried to damage your shield or make you abandon it? How do we protect our shield and not allow people to use it against us?

Things happen in life because it's "life," of course, but we have options to help ward some of those things off. We have tools, and better yet, we have a shield.

Keep your shield in great shape, and don't let anyone deem your shield useless. If yoga is your shield, and the Bible is someone else's, so be it. What gets one person through a battle may not be what gets another through their battle. What's most important is that your shield helps you win.

What happens when your shield is damaged? You must be able to hit the 'reset' button in life, but when your shield is damaged, that makes it all the more difficult. Sometimes our insecurities or our vulnerability will play a part in allowing our shield to get damaged. Are you fighting through life now with a damaged shield? If so, it's time you polish it up and put it back into battle.

Perhaps it wouldn't be a bad idea to have multiple shields. When one is damaged, you can pull out another to help you get back on track.

Hopefully, you're not saying that you don't have a shield, because I'm almost certain you have something that helps you feel good. Something that allows you to feel on top. Something that helps you block attacks. I'm not saying you have the right shield or the healthiest shield, but we all have one. You may need to fine tune your shield to ensure it's in position and shape to protect you.

We discussed mindfulness in chapter three with Daredevil. Mindfulness is my shield. Whenever I'm under attack, I find spaces around me where I can go to return to a mindful mindset. It brings me back to life, and reminds me that I'm untouchable, that I'm indestructible. Mindfulness is my reset button.

Knowing where your strength comes from is your responsibility. Knowing what you can do to hit the reset button is your responsibility. In this book, I'm giving you the tools to reach your true potential. I'm sharing the blueprint. It's up to you to use it to continue to build.

Discover Your Superpowers

CHAPTER 14
DON'T OBSESS OVER THE PAST

Wolverine, a mutant with enhanced physical abilities, was allegedly born in 1880. His real name is James Howlett, but he later took on the name Logan. There was no chemical spill or any type of explosion that resulted in his superhuman abilities; Wolverine was born with his superpowers. Humph . . . imagine that. Born a superhero. Go figure.

At some point, he was recruited by a military scientist to undergo a procedure that would line the skeleton of his body with adamantium. Adamantium is a metal alloy (fictional, of course). It's next to impossible to destroy. Wolverine's quick healing abilities, another superpower he was born with, allowed him to survive the procedure. After the procedure was over, he had no memories of his past; therefore, he spends his entire life searching for answers.

Entire life.

Searching.

For answers.

Not knowing may be one of the hardest things a human may ever endure. It's mental torment. Is he cheating? Is she cheating? Why did they leave me? Who killed them? How did they die? Why did they kill themselves? Why did they do it? Who is my father? Why did my mother give me away?

Not knowing causes a constant void. It's a huge hole that sucks up both one's conscious and sub-conscious. It's mentally crippling. Having to function like this on a day-to-day basis can be exhausting, robbing one of being able to enjoy life's moments . . . not being able to enjoy the present or look forward to the future because every waking moment is spent with concern about the past.

The irony of it all is that while some people claim they wish they could forget their past, they commit so many years of their life dwelling on it. And for some reason, humans tend to choose to dwell on the negative events of the past rather than the good. We do have a choice, you know.

The past. The past should not automatically be

looked at with a negative connotation. That only happens when one chooses to dwell only on the negative things of the past. We all have choices when it comes to what we want to fill our minds with. What do you choose to fill your mind with, the good stuff or the bad stuff? Maybe even a little mixture of both?

Wolverine's past consisted of him being neglected by his mother after she suffered from the death of her first son. I imagine he wondered why his mother didn't want him . . . want to take care of him. Why wasn't he enough? Why couldn't he make her happy? Sounds like a past one might want to forget, but you don't know what you don't know, never once considering that not knowing may be the gift, while knowing what is far too much to bear is the curse.

It's human instinct to want to know "what happened." Have you ever watched one of those crime solving shows, only to find that on that particular episode, the crime doesn't get solved? An entire hour with no resolve whatsoever. So just imagine living an entire lifetime with no resolve.

Wolverine's obsession with figuring out his past is his weakness. How many people do you know with that same weakness?

Living in the past or allowing your past to define

you can rob you of life. Not only does constantly focusing on the past mean you are not present, it's a distraction. I agree that there are some things in the past that are beneficial to know, but those things that will not serve you and are irrelevant should be let go.

The past is gone, the future isn't guaranteed, so now equals FREEDOM! Release yourself from the imprisonment of the past. Allow yourself the freedom to live in the moment.

Wolverine has the power of self-healing, but, in my opinion, he does not use it to the fullest. Sure, he may use it to restore physical injuries, but what about the restoration of his mind? Why doesn't he utilize his power of self-healing to heal himself?

The power of self-healing, I believe, is a gift we each have inside of us, but just like with Wolverine, we don't always use it. We can use this gift to heal from the past, from our past mistakes, to forgive ourselves, to ask for forgiveness, and to forgive others.

We all have a person or people in our lives who have challenged us. That challenge shows up in many forms such as hurt, disappointment, abandonment, feeling left out, and so on. But now, lucky for you and them, you will have the power to self-heal.

I used the power to self-heal a few times in my life, but one particular time was going into my adulthood. I was holding onto some hurt because of my past relationship with my father and it showed up as anger. I know this message will tap into a lot of your souls, and I hope you embed the message into your mind because it can be life-changing.

My parents were young when I was born. My father had a hard time with the fact that he was so young and had to be a father; responsible for another life. Heck, someone was still responsible for his! In my mind, I felt I was his first big mistake in life, and he verbalized these sentiments a time or two.

There are times in our lives when we think people are responding to us negatively because of what they say, do, or perhaps don't do or say. In most cases, it has nothing to do with us.

Have you ever taken something personally, then you realize it had nothing to do with you at all? You find that the person is responding to what they know, how they know to respond, the way they were taught to respond or act. Everyone has their own movie playing in their head and it's based on their individual experiences. Most of their experiences were set or planted into their conscious prior to their involvement with you. It's quite egotistical, actually, the way our minds work, because as humans we tend to shift things to be about ourselves very easily. Lucky for us, we have superpowers to help conquer these feelings of hurt and pain.

I recall my cousin giving me a piece of advice that was so powerful. I've shared this advice with multiple people throughout the past years, and it's changed relationships and perspectives. He told me a story about one of his loved ones and how he had to learn to take the title off their name, because titles come with expectations. He said taking titles off of people allows you to see the person for who they are and not for who you expect them to be.

WOW! Did you read that? Read it again: Take the title off of people's names, because titles come with expectations. Remember, they aren't the only person with a movie in their head. You have a movie in your head, too, and your expectations of others are based around what you've seen, believe, feel and need. You might base your expectation off of *The Cosby Show* or *Growing Pains*, which has skewed your perspective. Needless to say, I have used this practice in my life on multiple occasions, and it's a self-healing tool everyone needs to learn.

By doing this, it will allow you to see people

as human, and we all know what tendencies we as humans have. It will allow you to turn hurt into forgiveness, and by forgiving, you heal yourself. Forgiveness allows you to walk through life without anger, resentment, or bitterness, because at the end of the day, you typically are the only one feeling that way. Be protective of your energy and release those negative feelings.

I had my own set of expectations of my father, which created the relationship we had. Did he have his part in the creation? Of course, but I'm only responsible for my part, just like you're only responsible for your part in a relationship. Forgive yourself right now for ever allowing someone else to affect you to the point where it is toxic for only you. This technique taught to me by my cousin transformed my relationship with my father into one that I value and respect.

Even though Wolverine was born with superpowers, he wasn't able to heal his mind. So remember, no matter what superpowers you possess, if you can't let go of the past and be at peace, they won't bring you the greatness they are supposed to.

How can you stay mindful throughout life if you're holding onto hurt, pain, abuse, or abandonment from your past? Let the past go so you don't miss opportunities that are right in front of you; opportunities that could lead to great memories of what's yet to come!

CHAPTER 15
You're Worth It!

Out of all the superheroes I address in this book, Luke Cage may be one of the lesser known. Perhaps even a less memorable character in comparison to Superman, Wonder Woman, Batman, and the Hulk. But that doesn't make him any less of a superhero. There are probably others in your field or profession who are more well-known than you. That doesn't take away from who you are and what you are capable of accomplishing.

As a youngster, Luke Cage, then known as Carl Lucas, was a member of the notorious gang, The Bloods. He was born in Harlem, New York where he spent most of his teen years in and out of juvenile homes. This, of course, was a result of his gang related activity, along with engaging in crimes such as petty theft.

I know what you're thinking; that this description doesn't fit that of someone we would consider a superhero. Sounds more like one of the villains that a superhero would take out, huh? But do you agree that no matter where he came from, no matter how his life started out, no matter what type of person he used to be, it shouldn't take away from who he is today?

"But Luke Cage is just a fictional character, Tam," some of you might be saying. "In the real world, a leopard never changes his spots." For anyone who may be thinking that, perhaps you never heard of Reginald Dwayne Betts. Mr. Betts served eight years in prison after committing a carjacking when he was only 16 years old. Once released, he became one of the rare convicted felons to get a law degree from Yale, and then went on to pass the Connecticut bar exam. How's that for the real world? Like a friend of mine always says: "Your past may be the foundation of and what led you to your present, but your future is determined by your right now . . . not your yesterday."

Do you know someone with rough and sketchy beginnings? Maybe they didn't always do the right thing or make the right choices in their past, but they've learned and grown from it, today making them someone that others can learn from. I know someone who was in and out of jail growing up, but now they are helping and mentoring others to keep from following in their footsteps. They can speak from experience, being transparent, and an example of how it's never too late for one to change for the better.

How can people *not* change? Is it even possible to always be the same person throughout life? After all, you're not the same person today as you were in your teen years, are you? This is why I'm often disturbed when watching television and we see someone perform a heroic act, but then the next day someone has dug up something from the hero's past to try to destroy the image of the person. People change, and are expected to change, especially with age. If prison is supposed to be a place for "rehabilitation," why then does the very institution that created "the system" not believe in its own mission and purpose? Why would we expect a person to exit prison and enter society being anything other than a better person? Does this always happen? Of course not, but I use this to prove my point.

It's possible that you weren't always the delightful, intelligent, law-abiding, productive citizen that you are today. Or maybe you were. My point is that it's important that we don't become fixated on who we (or someone else) used to be versus who we (they) are today, and their full potential for tomorrow.

Like Carl Lucas, every day people sit back and take a look at some of the bad decisions they made in life—see how it could destroy their future and hurt their family and loved-ones—and decide to change for the better. It's who that person is today and will be tomorrow that matters most, not who they were yesterday.

But sometimes it seems that no matter how hard we may try to change and how much we actually do change, there is always that one person who tries to keep us from becoming better. This was the case with Carl and his old buddy, Willis Stryker, who even after Carl gave up the life of crime, he stayed friends with (even though Stryker remained in the life of crime). But it was Stryker, Carl's so-called friend, who was responsible for Carl eventually ending up in jail after Stryker planted drugs in Carl's apartment and then tipped off the police.

While incarcerated, Carl became the subject of an experiment that was purposely intercepted, hoping it would kill him. Instead of killing Carl, it gave him superhuman strength, durability, and unbreakable skin. Carl used his newfound superpowers to break free from jail. But let me give this to Carl; sometimes we have to break free from our old selves. The old you and me can remain imprisoned in the past, but the new you and me deserves freedom.

Carl uses his freedom to return to Harlem and rebuild his life. He takes on the alias of Luke Cage. Have you ever thought of taking on an alias, a new name, like Carl did? Not necessarily do a legal name change, but change your mindset so that whoever you were in your past (old mindset) becomes replaceable by who you have become (new mindset).

But as life goes, even with his alias and new mindset, Luke is confronted by his past. Sometimes, when a dark past haunts us, we have to clear our name, and we do so by being honorable, trustworthy, and integral, which is what Luke did. Don't allow that old you to confront the new you on a daily basis; having you question who you really are to the point where you feel like a fraud. I, like everyone else, have a past, but like the book says, "I Ain't Me No More."

Of course, there are those who will always and forever only remember the past you. I call those kinds of people the "Remember Whens." They are constantly trying to remind you and society to remember when you used to do "this" or remember when you used to do "that." Granted, it can sting sometimes, but like Luke Cage, we must have tough skin. Not everyone will be for us, for our change, or support our ideas, accomplishments, or our journey in general. We'll get talked about, lied on, and have our past held against us, even after we clear our names.

The same way Luke Cage has unbreakable skin, AKA "thick skin," so must we in life. This will allow us to continue on our path to purpose without getting injured. But the skin can't be so thick that it becomes a barrier. Building walls so that you can't get hurt could mean that when you are hurt, there is no one to help you. Some of the boundaries you have set up may not only be keeping you safe; they may keep others out completely. This may be a good strategy to minimize loss of love, safety, and belonging, but when you need someone, no one will be there or they won't be able to get through to you. Having thick skin and certain boundaries in place is a necessity, but unscalable walls could lead to isolation and seclusion.

What makes Luke Cage different than most superheroes is that his superpowers are for hire. If his price can be met, he'll save the day. That may not seem noble or integral, but isn't that the way of life? Don't most people charge for the utilization of their skills? And that's quite okay.

I've met several entrepreneurs who love and are passionate about what they do, but they have a hard time putting a price tag on it. They constantly lowball themselves when it comes to pricing. They constantly offer discounts, or they end up doing tasks for free. I get loving your job so much that you'd do it whether you got paid or not, but like literary educator Joylynn M. Ross says, "Just because you would do something whether you got paid or not doesn't mean you shouldn't get paid to do it."

Look at who you are today and all that you've accomplished. You are invaluable with so much to contribute to the world. Continue to labor in what you excel or strive to excel in, and don't hesitate to reap the fruits of your labor. You're worth it!

Discover Your Superpowers

CHAPTER 16
SERVICE

*H*ow many times have we packed up the food, packed up the kids, packed up the dog, and headed to the park in our minivan to enjoy a lovely picnic, only for drops of rain to begin greeting the windshield? It's at those moments—and outdoor weddings—that we wish we could control the weather.

Born Ororo Munroe, mutant to a tribal princess of Kenya and an American photojournalist father, in her superhero form, Storm can actually control the weather. Guess you know who to invite to your next picnic . . .

Raised in Manhattan, Storm was orphaned when her parents were killed in a bombing due to an Arab-Israeli conflict.

Storm was buried under rubble next to her mother's body, which is why she suffers from severe claustrophobia. Isn't it ironic that what we tend to suffer from today is usually a result of something we experienced in our past? This is why letting go of the past is such a challenge for some; there is a remnant (physical or psychological reminder) that acts as a constant connector.

Storm is discovered by Professor X of the X-Men and he convinces her to put her powers toward a purpose. She becomes a teacher at the mutant school and leader of the X-Men. What's so noble about Storm is that she becomes sort of a role model and example to those who want to become part of the X-Men. She teaches the young mutants how to use their powers. She gave back by providing a service to make others better.

Here we have a leader who could remain the biggest person in the room—the person with the most abilities—deciding to teach others what she knows. After all, there are so many people who have great gifts, but they have no idea how to use them. Often, they need others to teach them how to put their skills to use, and to help them discover (bring attention to) their skills.

I mentioned my superpower of seeing potential in you that you don't see in yourself; I help unearth it and bring it out. I'm giving back by helping each and every one of you. If you're reading this book, then I know you have the capacity to reach your true potential.

I connect with Storm more than any superhero, because my mission is similar. I'm a superhero, and it's my mission to make sure you know that you are a superhero too. I'm a superhero who gets to train other superheroes. Now that's empowerment. I'm living the dream!

We can't be afraid to teach others what we know, fearing they may grow to be better than us, more popular than us, or make more money than us. When in the role of teacher, our mission should be to make sure the student becomes better than us. Just like with parenting; we should want to teach our children to be better than us.

Raising the standards and raising the bar with one another is what allows us to grow. Operating on the "I taught you everything you know, not everything *I* know" mantra is why so many people become stifled and don't progress. But in the role of student, we also have to use discernment and know when our season is up with someone . . . when we have nothing else to learn from them. And of course, in teacher role, we must discern when we have nothing left to teach. In the coaching world, we have to be mindful of when we've piqued in a consulting or coaching relationship; otherwise, we are holding someone's success hostage. No individual's success should be at the mercy of another individual's . . . ever. It's unfair to make someone feel as if they can't succeed without you, your skills, and your guidance.

What's fascinating about Storm is that she can fly, but not due to her superpowers. What allows her to fly is that she can create storms strong enough to carry her weight. Okay, so it's indirectly as a result of her superpowers, but it's always good when a person can carry their own weight and not have to always depend on others. That goes back to knowing when our season is up with someone; not being dependent on them.

There is power in serving others, and not just for the other person. You can transform negative thoughts of yourself into positive, happy, and satisfied thoughts of yourself simply by serving others. Serving can allow you to go from failure to gratitude in a matter of minutes. You've heard of a gratitude journal, haven't you? A gratitude journal is a list of things you write down that make you feel grateful. It's a list to remind you to be grateful, and that you have more to be grateful for than not. Having gratitude embedded in your heart is another superpower it would serve you (and the world) best to stake claim of.

I recently learned about the law of nature. The principle is if someone comes into your life and needs help and you do all you can to help them, that something great will happen for you within seven days. It's the same principle as giving and receiving. If you are struggling with concerns and fears, why not try some of these techniques to help take the focus off yourself and onto someone else? Experience the great joy you can get from giving and serving–It will be greater than the agony and pain of focusing only on yourself.

My mother has always had a soft spot for the elderly. She gives them her time and serves them. She says you can never have a day that's bad when you've helped an elderly person's day to be better. She says helping the elderly makes her days feel good even when someone else would classify it as bad.

Change isn't easy, and perhaps you've been pretty selfish throughout your life. (Excuse my candidness, but I'm just keeping it real with you.) We all have the tendency to be selfish, myself included. If you can find it in your heart to expand your willingness to serve, you can reap long-term rewards. Ask yourself, "Have I done anything for someone else lately?"

I'm a stickler for practicing what I preach. I don't just talk the talk, but I walk the walk. I'm serving by opening up my heart to help people dream. I'm serving by sharing the messages in my head and heart that I know aren't solely meant for me.

My friends call me the wise one. I don't have all this information floating in my head just to keep it to myself. I'm serving . . . I'm teaching. It's what I'm here for. It's why I was born. I get messages in my mind that I know aren't for me at all, but to share with someone else for their benefit. Some of those messages are penned inside this book. I'd be extremely selfish not to share it with you. I'm serving today. I want you to decide who you're going to serve tomorrow.

CHAPTER 17
SHINING WITHOUT BEING THE STAR: KNOW WHO YOUR ROBIN IS

Richard John Grayson was the youngest in a family of Gotham City acrobats known as the Flying Graysons. In a mafia's boss attempt to extort money from the circus that employs the Flying Graysons, Richard's parents are killed while he watches the tragedy take place.

Bruce Wayne, aka Batman meets Richard while investigating the case, and takes him under his wing (literally 😊). Bruce legally adopts Richard, with Richard becoming Bruce's partner in crime-fighting. Richard becomes known as Robin, Batman's wingman, always there when Batman is in a bind. Besides his acrobatic stunts, he doesn't have any other superpowers. For that reason, people tend not to look at Robin as anything more than Batman's—the real superhero—sidekick.

But even if that were the case, there is no shame in being someone's sidekick, roadie, right-hand, man (or woman), or their ride or die partner. Their road dawg. The person they can depend on no matter the circumstance, crisis, situation, or celebration.

It takes the work of an entire team to make the dream work; to complete tasks successfully. Team members must serve a purpose, one that their skills line up with and can fulfill. But not everyone on the team can be the captain, though, as not everyone is equipped to lead. There have to be players in order to form a team. If everyone is a captain, then that ultimately results in an "every man for himself" mentality. It doesn't matter how great the captain is, he can't win alone. Let's take for example, LeBron James in game one of the 2018 NBA Finals. Known as the greatest basketball player ever, he played his heart out. He gave it his all on his mission to strive for the win. He outscored everyone to the point that he broke records. But his team didn't win. All that he did, as hard as he worked, as much as he stood out, as bright as he shined, his team didn't win.

No one can win on their own, as the scenario I

just gave you proves. LeBron's teammates worked hard as well. It was because of their skills that LeBron was able to excel in the manner he did. LeBron was able to depend on them to position him for greatness. And guess what? There is honor in being that dependable individual that people can count on, win or lose.

Leaders need a strong support system. Even the President of the United States of America doesn't run the country alone. I think that's why I'm not particularly fond of the word 'solopreneur.' That gives the impression that a person is building alone. I've never met an entrepreneur, business owner, or business founder who has done it all on their own. Whether it's the support of family and friends, outsourcing web design, editing, funnel building, or what have you, I guarantee someone else played a role in the laying of the bricks.

If you are in a position of leadership, who is your Robin? Who can you depend on to help you succeed? Still climbing the ladder of success? Whose Robin are you? Who can always depend on you to help them win? Even if you are in a position of leadership, that doesn't mean you still aren't someone else's Robin. Life doesn't always allow us to be everything to everybody, but we can be something to somebody.

If you want to win, there has to be that one go-to person that's working just as hard as you to bring home the championship trophy. I ask who's your Robin because it only takes one on your side to do some damage with. I, fortunately, have multiple Robins. It depends on what area of my life I'm fighting as to who responds.

Robin is a superhero who is "only human," just like you and me, yet he manages to be a master in different areas, earning him the title of "The Boy Wonder." No, Robin isn't built with the physique of Batman, but his own slender build allows him to respond more effectively in battle. We're all built to withstand different things in life. So, although Batman is the one in the spotlight, Robin still figures out a way to shine. And with his brilliance and investigative skills, Robin has the potential to surpass Batman in the area of being a detective. That's what happens when you learn from the best and are fortunate enough to be able to sit at the table with experts. How you look at that experience and what you do with it is up to you.

CHAPTER 18
IMPORTANCE OF YOUR NETWORK

Although I've covered several individual superheroes, if you put most of them together, they form a team known as The Avengers. They become one network. Your network will impact the way you think, act, and feel on a day-to-day basis.

In my early 20s, I started taking a critical look at my network; the people I was surrounding myself with. My road dawgs, clique, circle, tribe, friends, ride or dies. I recall having meetings called "homey meetings." I'm laughing as I'm typing; but, hey, our meetings were serious. It was time for us to discuss side projects we could do to expand our visions, dreams, and pockets.

Time is precious. Time is money. Time is

priceless. Time freedom is as equally as important as financial freedom. So, I had to be mindful of who I was spending my time with.

Allow me to be honest—I did more than simply take a look at my network, I analyzed the people in my life (friend, family, or foe). What did the conversations we were having sound like? What were some of the activities we were participating in? Were the people in my life adding to or subtracting from me?

Around the same time that I was taking inventory of my circle, I examined the relationship of a dear friend, and I started feeling as if she had possibly served her purpose in my life; that her season with me—or my season with her—was up. There is such a thing as a seasonal friend versus a lifetime friend.

I had and still have great love for this person, but our joint path was starting to separate to the point where I found myself headed in one direction and she in another. Some of you may describe that as slipping away, but no, this was no slip . . . no accident. I was heading—on purpose—in a specific direction. It just so happened that it was opposite of the one she was heading in. I won't say that this revelation was solely based on my inventory results. I'd had a couple incidences with my dear friend that led me to believe I needed to end our friendship. But even after I evaluated everything, there was a final situation that caused me to completely close the door.

Back then, I had a two-bedroom apartment. I'd landed a job as a sales rep and had just purchased a silver Chrysler Sebring convertible. Her envy began to spiral out of control. To this day, I still remember my parting words when we decided to honor our individual life's paths. "If you're jealous of me now, you're going to hate me later. So, we should end this now." And so we did.

Like I said earlier, I still love this person dearly. Just because you love someone doesn't mean you have to entertain their company, especially if their company, their energy and presence, stands a chance at stalling or stifling your success.

Success is relative! It's all about what makes you feel successful and whether you've reached your individual goals. Even back in my 20s, I had established a measure of success for myself. I knew then and I know now what's going to make me feel successful. But during the time when I parted ways with my friend, I was far from what success meant to me, so I was hurt and confused by her actions. A car? A two-bedroom apartment? A decent job? I realize now that those things may absolutely be someone's measure of success—they simply weren't mine.

Although at that time in my life I didn't feel like a failure—I was taking the necessary steps toward what *I* deemed as success. It's funny how what looked like success on me to others, wasn't what I deemed success. I mean, what if I'd really wanted a Jaguar and had to settle for a Sebring?

To others—at least to my then close friend—I looked successful. Regardless, I was in tune enough with myself and the things I wanted to achieve in life to know that I had to increase my circle of influence. This was a time in my life when I was still trying to figure things out, but I knew my network needed some fine tuning. Some minor adjustments definitely needed to be made.

Over the years I've constantly tweaked or adjusted my network with not much hesitation to adding or subtracting. Your network is precious and can make or break you, and your network will not and should not remain the same throughout your life journey. I recently had to part ways with a business partner. I haven't put much energy into the thought of parting ways with her. This may sound abnormal, or even a little cold, but knowing when to add and subtract people into my life is one of my superpowers.

Unfortunately, our business partnership ended on a sour note, which was a result of me no longer being able to trust her. It takes a lifetime to build trust, and a millisecond to ruin it. Broken trust ruined our business relationship. But the four years I was in business with her were some of the best years of my life. The day I met her was supposed to happen. I've learned more in the last four years about business than I ever would have if I had not met her. And the last four years were fun, exciting, and life-changing. She served her part in my life for a season, and now it's onto the next season! Ultimately, subtracting my former business partner made room for my new partners.

Don't get me wrong. I've had some amazing people in my network, but there were some missing components. I recall at one point making some phone calls to people I considered to be movers and shakers in my city to find out where I needed to physically be to surround myself with certain networks. I remember calling a doctor friend of mine in my network and she told me to go to Mike's house parties. Mike was known for throwing parties and get-togethers. Always in attendance were people who were doing big things in their life; from people who were in college with a direction for themselves, to business owners who were mentors to others. There are people in your life who can tell you exactly where you need to be and what time it starts—just ask them.

In rebuilding (or perhaps I should say remodeling) my network of people, one important factor was surrounding myself with like-minded individuals; people who understood the path I was on regarding education and career; people who were already business owners. If I was going to be a superhero, then I needed to surround myself with other superheroes. It was important that I was around others who were achieving or had already achieved things I desired to, but didn't make me feel inferior. You don't want to be around a person who is smarter than you, and makes you feel stupid.

Being around superheroes who are smarter than you are gives you the opportunity to learn. It's not a moment to feel inferior because of the that fact you don't have the same educational opportunities. This is a time to get educated on subjects you are unfamiliar with or want to learn more about. Someone recently told me that if you're the smartest person in the room, then you're in the wrong room. Don't be afraid to upgrade your network!

When talking about being rich and wealthy, it's not always about money or material things, but for the sake of this particular moment in this chapter, it is. Being around superheroes who are better off financially or have more material things than you gives you an opportunity to dream. I remember going into people's homes and leaving in awe thinking, "*What do I need to do in order to get here? What changes or slight adjustments do I need to make to ensure I experience life the way I want to experience it?*"

Having superheroes who are mentally stronger than you in your network not only gives you hope for your own life situations that you may encounter, but it pushes you and encourages you to keep pressing forward. Not to compare war scars, but just when we feel as if we've gone through something, we learn the next person's story and realize what we thought was a mountain was a molehill. Witnessing someone overcome adversity may just be the key to you getting through your own challenges.

Find that superhero who motivates you and makes you want to do bigger things and be better. The same person you want surrounding you in your network, you should strive to be that same individual in someone else's. I consider myself to have a lot of ambition, but when I met my husband, I had never met someone who inspired and motivated me the way he did. His work ethic and the pep talk I'd hear him giving himself always put a fire under me. He's still giving himself pep talks, by the way. He knows the importance of one having to encourage themselves. All the while, very few times does he realize he's killing two birds with one stone; he's encouraging both himself and me with that single pep talk.

If you haven't said it yourself, I'm sure you've heard someone else say, "I love a challenge!" It's quite easy to say that until you're actually faced with the challenge. But if your network consists of individuals who actually do challenge you, then when a challenge does come along, the battle is not as tough to win.

Who's your team? Who's your network? Are they people who are positive, uplifting, and encouraging? Do you have any negative individuals in your network?

Before you answer that last question, I think it's important that you don't confuse a negative person with the one who simply isn't afraid to tell you the truth. That person only willing to point out rainbows, unicorns, and penny candy can be potentially dangerous. That's the kind of person who tends to see no wrong in anything you do or say. You need people on your team who can put you in your place. It may not always be comfortable, but it's quite necessary.

Let's not forget about the superheroes who genuinely love you and will always have your back no matter what. I'm an only child, but I have sisters who love me. If all you get from this person is love, then keep them on your side. I'm a magnet for positive people, positive energy, and positive vibes. I remember my coworkers calling me "Positive Polly." I am what I attract. Who do you attract? In other words, who are you?

I've had people tell me that I see life through rose-colored glasses. I tell them my glasses are better than the poop-colored glasses they are looking through. I'm sorry, but I'm not exchanging my glasses. Some consider this my gift to their network. What's your role in your network? Because remember, being part of a network is about both giving and receiving.

Now, for those folks who actually are negative. Negative attitudes can drag you down, causing strife, discord, and confusion. As much as we may try to detach ourselves from negative people, every now and then someone is just having a bad day, and whom do they decide to call to be their sounding board? You, of course!

How do you feel when you hang up the phone after engaging in a negative conversation?

Sometimes it can take some time to shake it off. Surrounding yourself with negative people can bog you down emotionally and physically. Choose to not spend your time in that space. You do have a choice. That choice may simply be not answering the phone during the moments where you don't have the energy to give. It's okay to preserve your energy.

How comfortable are you with parting ways with the negative people who are subtracting from you? I need to be around dreamers. My stepfather dreams with me. My aunts dream with me. My cousins and I have the best dream sessions ever! We talk about vacations, ways to live our best lives, dream jobs, and business ideas. By the time we get off the phone, we are excited to go to work to make the dreams come true. One by one, I make my dreams come true, because I keep the dream close to my mind. It's on my vision board so I can visualize it. If it's in my mind and I can see it, then it's going to happen. Regardless if you dream in color or black and white—meaning it doesn't matter what the dream looks like—if you have the ability or capacity to dream, truly see it happening, then you can count on it to come to fruition.

Look at your team and network of people. Does your network offer you room to grow, or have you outgrown your network? Are those in your circle working for/with you or against you? Helping, hurting, adding, subtracting?

Your network is what you make it, because the great thing about it is that you have the right and the power to make it . . . to make it exactly what you want it to be.

I've met people in my lifetime who prefer being the lone wolf. They have a fear of blending in or getting lost in the crowd. It's your superpower that makes you stand out from every other superhero. What is your personal specialty? There are thousands of restaurants, but it's that specialty that makes each one stand out. You have it too; that special ingredient. In business, it's that something that gives you an edge on the competition.

Do you constantly have to be surrounded by others? Is it okay to do things apart from the collaborations with your team? Absolutely! Storm had to take a brief stint away from the X-Men. But remember, no man is an island. You need to be in alignment with at least one other superhero . . . your Robin.

I have superheroes in my family who are ready to respond. My parents, my grandparents, aunts, uncles, play sisters and brothers. And watch out for my cousins! I have my superhero friends who help me conquer this thing called life. I have my spiritual superheroes who pray for me and my family. Everywhere I turn, I'm surrounded by superheroes.

So, in closing out this chapter, it's my hope that not only have you uncovered the superhero in you, but in others as well. Find those who you can learn from, who motivate you, love you unconditionally, and who challenge you. Find your superheroes to take on this world with you. Build your team with those who will help you achieve your dreams and reach your true potential.

CHAPTER 19
LIMITED BELIEFS

Viewing life through your own movie lens is a great practice. Family, friends, coworkers, and church members all have their own 8mm film rolling through their head. Their own experiences, relationships, and education have shaped them into who they are and what they believe. They have their own way of thinking about things because of those experiences. Sometimes, without you even being aware, others' experiences and beliefs can be projected on you. At the same time, you can project yours on others. You have your own movie running in your head as well. When we become laser focused on that step and repeat reel, it's easy to ignore those things in our peripheral vision, or completely forget about things that may be in our blind spot.

It's important to create your own story and be true to it. Making bad decisions based on what has already played out in life is unacceptable. Things that have happened to you have already happened. It's your story. It's your truth. You can rewind and watch the scene play out again, but you can't revise it. What you can do, though, is change your perspective on it. Because know that in life, even when situations can't or don't change, that doesn't mean you can't change.

Some people have limited beliefs because of the movie playing out in their head . . . because of what is going on in their life and how they choose to act as a result. What role are you playing in life based on how you are acting out what's in your head? Next, determine what role you are playing in life based on what others may be viewing through their lens, which is based on their experiences and not yours.

Society projects their beliefs on us daily. This has always been done by the media, but now social media plays an even larger role. Now any and everybody can use their platform to instill their beliefs through YouTube videos, Instagram videos, Facebook, LinkedIn, articles, and blogs.

Parents have their beliefs that are projected on

us at a very young age. Then we have educators, school curriculum, laws, social norms, and the list goes on. We live in a world full of influencers. Just because you saw it, heard it, or was exposed to it doesn't give you an excuse to become it.

The media not only tells us stories, but then they, along with those with a platform, tell us how we should feel about the story. For example, people love bacon, but we are told it's not healthy, and if we must eat the fatty protein, then to only eat it for breakfast. Why? And who started that concept and ran with it to the point where they passed it on like it was a baton in a relay race?

Well, clearly there are enough bacon lovers out in the world who, in turn, took a stand and started their own campaign countering that belief. Now you can find ads for bacon ice cream, bacon with macaroni and cheese, bacon potato chips, and more. I mean, bacon ice cream? What a way to take a stand and counter a belief that was placed on society. Go bacon!

We are shaped by all of these beliefs, something as minor as giving up a food that we absolutely love. But what is true? Are those norms or beliefs authentic to you? Are you breaking out of that box to reach your true potential, or are you marching to the beat of someone else's movie soundtrack?

Make sure the movie in your head is your truth. Written, produced, directed by, and starring YOU! Don't play a secondary character in someone else's script. People are conquering their dreams every day. Take The Incredibles, for example.

What in the world do The Incredibles have to do with anything? Well, the animated family of superheroes battled trying to be silenced and stifled from using their superpowers.

The Incredibles were being asked to minimize themselves and fit in to being someone else's version of normal. Society shapes our thoughts as to what is good enough, and we live our lives trying to fit in that box. What if your goals and ambition don't fit in that box, or a box period for that matter? Do you reshape and shrink yourself to fit in the box anyway? Have you become a life contortionist?

Or perhaps you're on the opposite end of the spectrum. Do you judge others who don't live in the box you've put together like a piece of Ikea furniture? Is it possible that you fear others may excel beyond you if you don't keep them in that box? Is your truth that you are the influencer who others look up to, and you use your influence to project your insecurities and fears on others? That would be abuse of superpowers, you know!

Sorry (but not sorry) if I happen to step on a few toes during the process, but this book isn't your typical feel-good, self-help inspirational work of non-fiction. This is a resource to help you reach your true and full potential no matter how uncomfortable it may get. It's not always comfortable and it doesn't always feel safe to admit and accept your truth, but if you want this book to be most effective for your personal and business growth and development, it's something that isn't an option, but a necessity.

It's just you and the words in this book, so it's safe to identify your truth. No one else is listening. No one else will ever know your truth unless you decide to share it. But first, you must be open to search for your truth, embrace it, and then use it to your benefit. Eventually, maybe you'll even use it to benefit others as well.

In helping others by using your own experiences and beliefs, don't mix up *projection* with *protection*; the two are not interchangeable. For example, our family and friends can come off as protecting us by using their beliefs to persuade us to do or not to do certain things, but it can, in all actuality, simply be them projecting their own fears they've accepted for themselves. Projecting is easy to do and we've all done it a time or two, knowingly or unknowingly.

Have you ever told someone a plan of yours only for them to respond by saying, "Are you sure you want to do that?" or "Do you really believe that's a good idea?" What about the times when you've already taken a leap of faith? For example, you enrolled in that class that is going to better position you for a promotion, you can't wait to share the news, and when you do, what reply do you get? "Isn't that expensive? Are you sure you're going to be able to afford to do that?" or "Do you have enough time for a class? Your plate is already pretty full." This is their fear, not yours. Don't listen to them.

How many people do you know who are on some sort of mood or anxiety medication, or resort to self-medicating, even if it means utilizing illegal substances, all because they are trying to mask or numb themselves? Is this because we are too busy trying to be a character in someone else's movie but we never make the cut? Is this because of feeling like measuring up to society's expectations is too hard? It's not hard if we take time to make our own movie. Let people watch your movie instead of making a movie you think they want to watch. Are you performing for everyone? If so, it's exhausting and you'll feel relieved and happy when you stop tap dancing.

So, what are some ways to know whether or not your movie is a "YOU Original" production? Try picking through your brain to pull out the brainwashing or programming. Get out a pen and paper and make a list if need be. Begin to vanquish the weeds (others' thoughts or limited beliefs) and reveal that beautiful garden of YOU.

Are there times in life where you have to play background? Yes, but there is never a time where you should shrink yourself or become invisible. You are incredibly amazing and here for a reason. Take a moment to sit down to think critically about yourself. Turn off the TV, social media feed, or radio and change your mindset to listen to things that interest you instead.

Let's not be so quick to refer as those individuals who are stuck in a box as 'haters.' Again, there are those who honestly believe they are protecting you; looking out for you. But what they fail to realize is that they are projecting how they feel about themselves onto you. They may have a desire to go back to school, but not having enough time or money are excuses they've been feeding themselves. Now, subconsciously, they are projecting those fears and limited beliefs about themselves onto you. If there was ever a better time to go into superhero mode and pull out that shield, that would be the time. Your shield will provide protection from someone else's projection.

This is one of those cases when you have to be mindful of who you share your dreams and goals with. If someone can't see himself or herself stepping out of the box into their own movie, then how do you expect for them to see it for you? I'm not telling you to keep all of your dreams, visions, goals, and expectations for yourself and plans top secret. As mentioned in the previous chapter where we discussed the Avengers, find that like-minded person in your tribe who takes steps toward reaching their true potential, but who is not afraid to leap. Use that person as a sounding board.

People who are reaching their true potential are taking that leap of faith beyond their limited beliefs. The Incredibles reached their true potential because they didn't conform. They stuck to who they were and didn't walk onto anyone else's movie set.

If you haven't seen the movie *The Incredibles* take a Saturday afternoon and binge with your family and friends. You'll experience vicariously how happy it feels to just go for it and be yourself. Then you'll be filled with the courage to experience it firsthand for yourself.

Discover Your Superpowers

Sit down and play the movie that's in your head. Create, develop, and star in your own reality show. Edit out the beliefs that truly don't belong to you, leaving a production where you're not only the leading character, but where you have the power to cast your supporting characters as well. Just like The Incredibles, don't settle for living normal— somebody else's normal, that is. Live *your* normal, and all while reaching your true potential!

Discover Your Superpowers

CONCLUSION

*I*t's time to start leaping tall obstacles in a single bound. It's time to quantum leap from "only being human," to being a super terrific human who does super amazing things. It's time to uncover or start utilizing those things that make you super special . . . those things that make you a superhero.

Sometimes you have to filter through life's distractions to discover the greatness in you. In order to do so, if you have to clean up your life, so be it. Get to cleaning, my friend! Out with the old and in with the new. Because if you want to attract new things into your life, you need to free up space for them. Learn techniques to simplify your life. Uncover resources that will not only catapult you to amazing new levels in your personal life, family life, and career, but that will catapult others around you as well. Discern and be aware of better opportunities that can place you in better situations and circumstances.

Take a look at your surroundings. Use your environment to help begin preparing you for what's next. Align yourself with the energy that's already out there. Attract success instead of chasing after it, and stop struggling to reach your goals. Come up with a plan, set a timeline to achieve your goals, and take specific action steps to accomplish them. Yes, all of these techniques work. But what if I told you that you could also just have an intention, and based on that intention, what you want—what you desire—would manifest?

Well, that's exactly what I'm telling you, but I'd be doing you a disservice if I didn't also tell you that it takes work, both physically and mentally. Of all the things we work toward in life, the main one should be working to better ourselves and others. We should constantly either be learning something, teaching something, or meeting someone to help propel us to the next level.

As I've mentioned a couple of times, a superpower I've unearthed is that I see potential in people that they don't see in themselves. I'm a superhero who helps others identify themselves as superheroes while also identifying the powers that make them super. Everyone, and I do mean everyone, from the youngest child to elders, from a high school dropout to a scholar, is a superhero. I may not have x-ray vision, but my vision allows me to see beyond the surface of individuals to who they truly are and how they should be operating in and navigating the world.

I know it's not possible for me to meet every single person personally and help them along their superhero journey. But because I'm purposed and intent on helping as many people as I can, I have written and published this book, a companion journal and workbook, as well as online and in-person courses, all to be used as proverbial shovels to dig up the superhero that lives in you, and to dig up or dust off those superpowers that have been lying dormant. It's time to ignite your superpowers!

Sometimes we are quite aware of the superpowers we possess, but because we don't use them often enough, we forget we have them. Throughout each chapter, I asked several questions with the intent to give you something to think about. But during the process of the writing and publication of this book, I decided that giving you something to think about may not suffice. I'd like to give you something to write about, and even perhaps talk about. Allow the *Diary of a Superhero:*

Journaling Toward Your True Potential journal to serve as a tool to help you discover the superhero in you, uncover your superpowers, and learn how and/or start using them.

Once you've written your way to your true potential, start taking action to reach it with the *Work Your Way to Your True Potential* workbook. Then finally or simultaneously, join me in one of my courses or workshops. You can visit www.yourtruepotentialcoach.com to learn how to register.

But remember, just because you are this superhero with superpowers to take you to higher levels in life, even a superhero needs other superheroes. So, don't forget about forming your own superhero network. Your network should be a non-judgment and non-competition zone. People who love you and people who truly have your best interest in mind and at heart will not compare, compete, or judge. Your network should make you better, and you should make your network better, and collectively, using the quality of sharing, you may not be able to save the world, but you can change it . . . one superhero at a time!

About the Author

Tamara Paul is a graduate of Ohio University and has co-founded multiple companies. She's the CEO of Your True Potential, and CEO of Rep Network. Tamara Paul is a serial entrepreneur who wears many hats, so it's no surprise that she's added "published author" to her vast collection. Married to former NFL player, Tito Paul Sr., Tamara is a mother of two sons, Tito Paul II and Trey Paul.

Tamara brings to these companies a long track record in successful business management, including financial stability, corporate structure, operational frameworks, and process management. Outside of being the co-founder of Rep Network, Tamara serves as the company's Managing Partner for Finance and Operations. An experienced entrepreneur and small business owner, Tamara is the guru of organizational discipline and enablement.

Tamara has long recognized her greatest success is helping others succeed. As an independent network manager, she established an infrastructure to train and manage over 700 reps. She was highly regarded in her 13 years as a sales representative and territory manager for several of the world's leading pharmaceutical companies, frequently achieving top rankings for herself and her team. Her drive for cultivating entrepreneurial opportunities has also led her to build profitable businesses in real estate management, travel, equipment management, and entertainment. A former model, Tamara is an eloquent and energizing speaker on small business success.

A graduate of one of the most respected life and health coaching programs, Tamara is also a member of the International Coaching Federation. Her passionate commitment to her work focuses on personal and professional life coaching, health coaching, entrepreneurial consulting, work/life balance coaching, and inspirational speaking.

Tamara has a gift of empowering people to pursue their passions, increase self-confidence, live the life they truly want to live, and help them DREAM. To learn more about Tamara, connect with her or contact her, visit her website at www.authortamarapaul.com or www. yourtruepotentialcoach.com.

Follow Tamara and Your True Potential on social media:

LinkedIn (Tamara Paul) https://www.linkedin.com/in/tamara-paul-51510457/

Instagram (Tamara Paul) www.instagram.com/tamarapaul1

Facebook: https://www.facebook.com/Your-True-Potential

Twitter: @YTPotential

Instagram: www.instagram.com/ytpotential

LinkedIn: https://www.linkedin.com/company/yourtruepotential

Pinterest: www.pinterest.com/ytpotential

YouTube: https://www.youtube.com/channel/UCWIhHupRw5udWxRhp5dV_Ig

NOTES FROM CHAPTER 1

NOTES FROM CHAPTER 2

NOTES FROM CHAPTER 3

NOTES FROM CHAPTER 4

NOTES FROM CHAPTER 5

NOTES FROM CHAPTER 6

Discover Your Superpowers

NOTES FROM CHAPTER 7

NOTES FROM CHAPTER 8

NOTES FROM CHAPTER 9

Bonus Note Pages

NOTES FROM CHAPTER 10

NOTES FROM CHAPTER 11

215

Bonus Note Pages

NOTES FROM CHAPTER 12

NOTES FROM CHAPTER 13

Bonus Note Pages

NOTES FROM CHAPTER 14

NOTES FROM CHAPTER 15

NOTES FROM CHAPTER 16

NOTES FROM CHAPTER 17

Bonus Note Pages

NOTES FROM CHAPTER 18

NOTES FROM CHAPTER 19

Bonus Note Pages

Discover Your Superpowers

Discover Your Superpowers:

The Key to Unlocking Your True Potential

Order Form

PURCHASES CAN BE MADE USING THE ORDER FORM BELOW:

EMAIL ORDER FORM TO: BOOK@YTPOWERS.COM

FAX ORDER FORM TO: (614) 573-7297

MAIL ORDER FORM TO: 3982 POWELL RD. SUITE 148, POWELL, OHIO 43065

BILLING INFORMATION		SHIPPING INFORMATION (IF DIFFERENT)	
Name:		Name:	
Street:		Street:	
City:	Zip:	City:	Zip:
Country:		Country:	
Contact Name for Shipment:		Contact Name for Shipment:	
Phone:		Phone:	
E-Mail:		E-Mail:	

ORDER QUANTITY AND TOTAL		PAYMENT INFORMATION
Book Price:	$14.95	
Journal Price:	$19.95	
Workbook Price:	$13.95	
Quantity:		Method of Payment: Credit Card: ☐ Check Enclosed: ☐ Money Order Enclosed: ☐
		Credit Card #:
Subtotal (Book Price x Quantity):	$	Expiration Date:
Sales Taxes (if applicable):	$	CVC #:
Shipping & Handling (7% of subtotal; $6.00 minimum):	$	Name on Card (Please Print):

225

Bonus Note Pages

CPSIA information can be obtained
at www.ICGtesting.com
Printed in the USA
LVHW041135130119
603755LV00016B/339/P